DRENTHE
IN
MICHIGAN

DRENTHE
IN
MICHIGAN

H. J. Prakke

WILLIAM B. EERDMANS PUBLISHING COMPANY
for the

DUTCH-AMERICAN HISTORICAL COMMISSION
Grand Rapids and Holland

Contents

Acknowledgments

A number of people have been instrumental in making the translation and publication of *Drenthe in Michigan* a reality. They assisted in many ways, including translating, editing, proofreading, and obtaining illustrations and photographs.

Our sincere thanks to all these people: Ali and Don Riddering, Lenore and Herman Ridder, the staff and trustees of the Netherlands Museum, and members of the Dutch-American Historical Commission. Harry Boonstra provided the final draft of the translation.

Preface

The two Drenthes—a province in the Netherlands, and a community in Western Michigan—are linked by more than their identical name. In some respects the Drenthes are prototypes of countless emigrations that make up the American experience. This book examines in detail the genesis of one such emigrant movement.

To understand society's attitudes and events today—political, social, religious, and economic—requires knowledge of yesterday. Professor Prakke especially explores the yesterday of two Drenthes in this scholarly study. His work is thus a significant landmark because, except for a very early work by Van Hinte, Dutch historians have done little with the important mid-nineteenth-century emigration to mid-America.

Professor Prakke's interest in the experiences of the emigrants began in 1946, while he worked with colleagues, including me, to prepare for the 1947-1948 centennial observances of the American-Dutch settlement. During the Nazi occupation Holland's ties with the outside world, especially with the United States, had been severed. The sudden resumption of contacts with relatives and friends abroad, occasioned by the centennial, gave a great psychological lift to people on both sides of the Atlantic, and created a climate of personal awareness of both new and old values, as well as of family roots.

At the same time, residents who celebrated the centennial of their Dutch-American community were encouraged to study the history of its founding and origins. This stimulated further inquiry into the founders of Drenthe—to whom many modern Drenthians traced their ancestry.

Professor Prakke's grasp of the significance of the cultural ties of Dutch-American communities in America with the homeland is firm. As editor-publisher of the Van Gorcum Pers, Assen, he published the two-volume work *Dutch Immigrant Memoirs and Related Writings*, by the late Professor Henry Lucas. Also under his leadership the Drenthe Society commissioned a distinguished sculptor to create "The Seer." Placed in the wall of the town hall of Sleen, it serves as a memorial to the emigrants from Drenthe. A replica of this sculpture is in the Netherlands Museum in Holland, Michigan.

To readers who trace their ancestry to Drenthe, the Netherlands, as well as to readers who are intrigued by how their roots influence what they are today, I am happy to recommend an English translation of Professor Prakke's 1948 work in Dutch, *Drenthe in Michigan.*

Willard C. Wichers
Holland, Michigan

Spring 1982

Translation Notes

1. In translating Prakke we have sought to reproduce the original in idiomatic English, translating freely from the Dutch—while remaining faithful to the original. Those who know only English can judge if we have succeeded in producing idiomatic English; those who know both English and Dutch can determine if we have been faithful to the original.

2. We have omitted an occasional sentence or paragraph that was of purely local interest, which would be either of no discernable interest to American readers or unintelligible to non-Dutch readers, unless supplied with extensive background notes. If the omitted part consisted of a few words or names they were occasionally deleted silently. Usually the omitted material is indicated by bracketed ellipses [. . .].

3. The terms "Afgescheidenen" and "Gereformeerden" (only used a few times) have both been translated by "Secessionists." "Hervormd" has been translated by "Reformed" when referring to the Reformed tradition in the Netherlands; when designating the "state church," we have maintained *Hervormde Kerk.*

Prologue

"All things are full of weariness; a man cannot utter it; the eye is not satisfied with seeing, nor the ear filled with hearing." (Eccl. 1:8)[1]

A remarkable exception to the biblical statement that all things are in restless movement was the old village life in the Dutch province of Drenthe. At least it must seem so to those who wish to discover its nature through enthusiastic eulogists: *Laudatores temporis acti*. These eulogists (among whom I count myself) like to contrast the rural peace and tranquility of our ancestral villages of Drenthe with the hopelessly divided and fragmented life of the present; they also come with a fervent cry for more social cooperation or at least more positive action for the common good.

But what became of this idyllic community spirit when, more than a hundred years ago, several hundred inhabitants of this thinly populated province emigrated to North America? In the municipality of Sleen alone, nearly five percent of the population left.[2] According to confidential official reports at the time, they emigrated "because of religious reasons and a desire for improvement in their standard of living." To accomplish this purpose they joined the new colony in the State of Michigan, which their great leader, the Reverend Albertus C. van Raalte, named "Holland." The emigrants from the province of Drenthe founded their own settlement nearby, which they called "Drenthe."

This migration contradicts the conventional picture of the sedentary people of the province of Drenthe who would rather suffer poverty at home than seek prosperity elsewhere; it is inconsistent with the close-knit unity of these rural communities (for the most part they were inhabitants of the old villages in the sandy

ix

regions), and it contradicts their moderate religious consciousness. Indeed, this migration challenges all the standard character traits of the traditional Drenthian. Is this contradiction the reason that our American cousins have been neglected and almost forgotten in the Netherlands?

Last spring, when I called attention to the American Drenthe in the *Nieuwe Drentsche Courant*,[3] it became evident that it was more or less known in Reformed circles.[4] I received very nice responses, and at the founding of the "Drents Genootschap,"[5] people found the rediscovery of this godchild so interesting that we promptly sent off a telegram: "Old province of Drenthe Netherlands from where a century ago founders of your town came, send warmest greetings to American Drenthe and descendants of old Drenthe emigrants. . . ." It appeared to me as if we were sending a rocket to Mars during a favorable position of the stars (the centennial celebration of Holland, Michigan, 1847-1947), to ascertain if that planet were inhabited.[6]

As I considered this problem of the mass migration from those villages around 1847, it fascinated me more and more. If five percent would migrate from Amsterdam today, it would mean a mass departure of 35,000-40,000 people. But the five percent from the municipality of Sleen came primarily from the hamlet Erm. By a very conservative calculation this would mean about ten percent of the population of Erm. Again compared to Amsterdam, this would mean a group of more than 75,000 people all selling their belongings to establish a new community elsewhere.

It is obvious, then, that the static image of our ancestral rural communities must give way to the dynamics of a deeply cutting schism.

NOTES

1. The Dutch Bible verse is from the version *De Bijbel voor Huisgezinnen* ('sGravenhage, Erven Doorman en J. D. Steuerwald, 1841), also read in Drenthe at that time. The "List of Subscribers" includes, among others, J. A. Wijkstra Zwarts from Erm and A. V. L. Dinckgreve from Sleen.

2. From a population of 1,332 there were 59 who emigrated (according to Van der Scheer's *Drentsche Volksalmanak*, 1848).

3. Feb. 11, 1947.

4. I had become aware of the centennial through a poem in the weekly *Frysk en Frij*, Feb. 7, 1947.

5. On March 12, 1947, in the Statenzaal of the Provinciehuis in Assen.

6. The desired contact took place. One can notice the important role of the church in Drenthe, Michigan from the fact that our telegram was published in the "Church Bulletin." Miss Reta Kamps explained, "so everybody heard about it."

I

The Home-Bound Drenthian

DRENTHE MIGRATION THROUGH THE CENTURIES

"They hang on to old ways around here."
(A farmer from Drenthe, 1947)

The Issue

Through the centuries the social ties in the villages of Drenthe have been very strong, and to a large extent this is still true today. Even economic pressures can hardly persuade a villager to emigrate permanently. According to K. van der Kley:

> The historical isolation of Drenthe still has influence on its inhabitants. The typical person from Drenthe does not feel comfortable away from home. He feels strange, insignificant, and clumsy; he doesn't pull up stakes readily. On occasion he may take a job outside Drenthe, as a farmhand to the province of Holland, or as a miner to Germany or the province of Limburg. He and his wife may even settle there, but after a short time he returns. His wife may not feel at home in the strange place, or he may become homesick for his native land. Poverty had driven him away and this same deprivation will begin again after he returns. But he is content—he's home. (*Drentse Volkskarakter*)

"He doesn't pull up stakes readily." J. Poortman has some doubts about this supposed characteristic, and voices them in his

1

interesting article, "Steven Coerts, An Emigrant from Drenthe in 1660": "This does not exactly indicate a person stuck in his own village. . . . Years ago I protested in our local newspaper against this so-called characterization of staying put . . . . This shows that among the best who moved away to find a better, though unknown, future, the former inhabitants of Drenthe were not far behind in those dynamic times. At that time at least they were not stuck in a land that produced too little to feed everybody."

Was van der Kley wrong in his assertion regarding the past, or did the Drenthian attitude toward mobility change in the course of the years? Fortunately, van der Kley shows an awareness of the unusual nature of the migration to Michigan, although I believe that he underestimates the breadth and the significance of this movement. "At the time of the secession from the Dutch Reformed Church some families did emigrate to America. These settlements, however, were tightly-knit religious communities. The Drenthe emigrant did not find himself alone!"

A survey of the historical record will reveal how much is known about the emigration from Drenthe in the past few centuries.

Picardt

Dr. John Picardt, the first Drenthe historian (1600-1670), begins with a clear statement in his famous book *Antiquiteten.*

> It is true that in some towns of this province the Spaniards carried on in a horrible and barbarous manner; however, it didn't last very long and ended after a short, furious encounter. But Drenthe was on the rack, without reprieve, for at least one hundred and twenty years. How the people of Drenthe suffered from the Duke of Saxony! From the Count of East Friesland! [. . .] Notice the countless acres in Drenthe, formerly fertile grain fields, which are now lying waste, overgrown with dry heather. Notice also the estates with the houses burnt or destroyed. Notice the fields with roots and tree stumps, where oak forests were cut down in those troubled times. And notice the numerous generations of these people, as they were ejected from their own land, who went to other provinces to seek a fortune.

The military history of the sixteenth and seventeenth centuries shows us how long Drenthe suffered, since it was totally undefended, except for Coevorden. The Dutch historian P. C. Hooft says: "All the inhabitants were abandoned to the sword and fire of the occupation forces. The soldiers were allowed to treat them as they saw fit. Mischief, vandalism, and oppression were the result."[1] [. . .]

Professor Huizinga

The information in Picardt about the "fortune hunters in other provinces" is scarce. However, there is some evidence about contact between Drenthe and the city of Groningen, which was originally a settlement of Drenthe.

The famous historian Dr. J. Huizinga deals with the relationship between Drenthe and other provinces in his essay "The Patrician Oligarchy and the Immigration Into the City of Groningen Until About 1430."[2] "We can consider the city of Groningen, before it became a commercial center around 1100, as a settlement of Drenthe, in which the court of the bishop with its landed estates constituted a considerable part of the area. The rest of the property was largely held by independent farmers." In this study Professor Huizinga comes to the conclusion that "many of the ruling or wealthy families in Groningen originate from Drenthe." He continues:

> This in itself is not surprising; Drenthe, of course, supplied the most important contingent of immigrants. It is noteworthy, however, first, that some of these families, after having become citizens of Groningen, still maintained contact with Drenthe through feudal estates or family relationships; and, second, that the number of incoming Frisians was quite small compared to the number coming from Drenthe. This was probably because of the family relations: Groningen, which was originally settled by people from Drenthe, continued to attract people from Drenthe. Nevertheless, the opposite could also be expected, since Groningen had much more contact with Friesland.

Finally, Dr. Huizinga cites the remarkable description of the city, which the Ommelander nobleman Johan Rengers van ten Post published in his chronicle:

It has been built by lords and princes. It has not been a town for a long time, and there was in the beginning a flow of people from Drenthe, Westphalia, etc., who settled in Groningen. There they obtained rich and ample food and a good living from neighboring Frisia; all kinds of people were therefore drawn to this place.

The study then offers a number of examples.

Another statement by Professor Huizinga is also noteworthy: after 1400, Drenthe family names with *"van"* [i.e., "coming from"] continue to appear in the registers of the guilds. Many persons are named after the Drenthe communities of Beilen, Coeverden, Emmen, Odoorn, Anlo, Diever, Bork, Aalden, Valthe, Spijkerboor, Eelderwolde, Peizerwolde, and Roderwolde.[4] However, places of origin other than Drenthe also become more frequent.

Finally, Professor Huizinga points out the steady migration from the south to the north: "Many of the important Groningen families, some of them originating in Drenthe, soon obtained property in the *Ommelanden* [the regions north of Groningen that are now part of the province of Groningen] and partial or entire families moved there." Examples are the families of Polman, Sickinge, Kathers, Clanten, Rengers, and Marissinge.

Seventeenth Century

Settlers from Drenthe were also absorbed in the population of other neighboring regions, especially in the Saxon parts [Salland, Twente, and Graafschap Bentheim]. A striking example is found in the history of the family of Blijdenstein, originally from Bliestede (the present-day Ruinerwold). Berent and Adam Blijdenstein established themselves as hat makers in the Westphalian town of Burgsteinfurt, around the year 1600. Their religion, one assumes, was one of the important motives—they were Mennonites. Berent's widow later settled in Oostmarsum, from where one grandson moved to Enschede to become the ancestor of the rather numerous Blijdensteins of Twente (manufacturers of linen and cotton goods and bankers). The families of the Amsterdam shipowners Goedkoop and the Apeldoorn ink manufacturer Talens also came from Drenthe.

The adventures of another "fortune seeker" from seventeenth-century Drenthe were described by the historian Jan Poortman in the essay cited earlier: Steven Coerts van Voorhees (below Ruinen), who, at age sixty, emigrated with his family. In 1660 he traveled to New Amsterdam on the *Bonte Koe*. Twenty-nine of the forty-nine passengers came from Drenthe.

Poortman assumes that Coerts left Drenthe at his advanced age because of financial difficulties with his rental farm, and the realization that he could be evicted from house and land by anyone offering a higher rent. Coerts settled in America in New Amersfoort, where he bought a house, a barn, a brewery, and sixty acres of land. Four years later he was appointed a member of the local government (the same year in which the English took possession of "Nieuw Nederland"). In 1665 Governor Nicolls granted a charter to eight of the inhabitants of Amersfoort (Flatlands), in which their existing rights were acknowledged. Steven Coerts and his eldest son, Coert Stevens, were among these inhabitants. Van Voorhees, as the descendants later called themselves, became a famous family name in the New World.

[. . .]

Eighteenth Century

In the eighteenth century the "war-avoidance" policy of the Republic of the Seven Provinces gave a breathing spell to the inhabitants who stayed in the "Free Land of Drenthe." Little or nothing is known about emigration at that time. I did note an example of "Wanderlust" in *Maanblad Drente*.[5] In 1779 Roelof Otten Brunsting, born in Beilen, sailed as supply officer on the ship *Breedenhof*, "bound for Batavia" [Dutch East Indies], after he had passed his examination in Hoorn. A more important career at that time was that of another Drenthian: the son of the Governor of Drenthe, born in 1773, Lodewijk Graaf van Heiden van Reinestein. This supporter of the House of Orange left the country in 1794 as a young naval officer, to become, in Napoleonic times, an admiral in the Russian navy.

Were these the exceptions that prove the rule? "The people of Drenthe do not like to travel," van der Kley said.

The French Period

The French period brought Drenthe equality with the other provinces. There was greater mobility among the people and more individual emigration.

The improvement of public education in 1806, under the energetic leadership of Governor Petrus Hofstede, gave boys who wanted to study the opportunity to obtain diplomas. With these certificates they had the option of becoming schoolteachers outside their own province. My great-grandfather (born in 1795) left the family farm in Ruinerwold (still named the *Prakkerij*) to one of his brothers-in-law, although he was the only son of an ancient family of Drenthe farmers. With his teacher's certificate, which he earned in Assen, he settled permanently in Eibergen (Gelderland), as the principal of a school for forty years. In his school, French, German, music, and drawing were taught. It is remarkable that none of his numerous descendants ever returned to farming.

Nineteenth Century: The "Trek" of 1846-1847

We have seen that there was more individual emigration as a result of the integration of Drenthe into the State. The nineteenth century would soon give evidence of important group-emigration. And this brings us to the emigration which is of special interest in this study, namely, the great van Raalte Trek of 1847. We are, fortunately, in possession of important details about the emigration of 1845-1847, thanks to confidential reports that were submitted at that time to the Governor of Drenthe, Mr. J. A. G. Baron de Vos van Steenwijk.⁶

The very form of the request for one such report is interesting in itself. It was marked: "Cabinet - Confidential" and was sent to the mayors of Drenthe on February 8 (just one day before the first people arrived at the location where Holland, Michigan, was to be founded).

The questionnaire reads as follows:

It has come to my attention that for some time newspapers have been reporting that in the southeastern part of Drenthe many inhabitants are preparing to leave their country next spring to sail to North America, after having sold their possessions in this country.

Although I do not consider this emigration as important as other people seem to, I do believe it sufficiently important that I should know to what extent the information given is true, and for this reason I am requesting you honorable officials kindly to let me know confidentially the following matters:

1. Are there indeed inhabitants in your municipality who are making preparations to leave for North America next spring, and if so, how large is their number?

2. Is it known for what reasons these people are emigrating?

3. To what religious persuasion does the majority belong?

4. Is this emigration limited to the working class and those of moderate means or does it also pertain to the wealthier class; also, can one ascertain whether these people are being encouraged to emigrate? And, finally,

5. Have any other inhabitants of your municipality already left for North America and, if possible, can you tell me the number of these people?

The regional enquiry was followed by another one on the initiative of the Assen branch of an influential association, *De Maatschappij tot Nut van 't Algemeen* (according to a government release of November 25, 1847).

The final request for information was a resolution from the Governor of Drenthe, dated January 20, 1848 (initiated by the Minister of Home Affairs at The Hague.)[7] In this request the municipalities were asked to submit an additional report with "the names and first names of the emigrated heads of families and of the bachelors, and their ages, and in addition whether they were liable for any taxes, and if so, in which class; whether these emigrants were accompanied by their wives, children, and servants and, if this was the case, how many; and, finally, where they had moved to."

The municipalities involved in this emigration appeared to be Assen, Coevorden, Beilen, Borger, Dalen, Zwingeloo, Emmen, Havelte, Hoogeveen, Odoorn, Rolde, Ruinerwold, Sleen, Smilde, Westerbork, Zuidlaren, and Zeeloo. Apparently there were no emigrants from Anlo, Diever, Eelde, Gasselte, Gieten, Meppel, Norg, Nijeveen, Oosterhesselen, Peize, Roden, Ruinen, Vledder, Vries, De Wijk, and Zuidwolde. (For the location of this emigration movement see the map on page 4.)

1845: Roman Catholic Emigrants

The emigrants who left in 1845 are not shown on the map on page 4; they form a separate group. They were farmers with their families, the mother-in-law of one of them, with two children and one farmhand with his family; altogether there were thirty-six emigrants, all from Nieuw Schoonebeek (at that time part of the Dalen municipality; Schoonebeek did not become an independent municipality until 1884). All were Roman Catholics.

The heads of three of the families were considered prosperous, and two of moderate means. The average age of these five heads was thirty-six. The probable reason for their moving was the hope of a more prosperous existence.

Upon request the local officials reported in 1848 that these emigrants had established themselves in Michigan in the year 1845. We tend to put a question mark here: did they reach Michigan before the Reverend van Raalte arrived there? Van Raalte did meet

"Catholic Dutchmen" in Buffalo in 1846. Dr. van Hinte, in his book *Nederlanders in America* (in the chapter dealing with Catholic emigration in those years), mentions that the oldest emigration was the one from the North Holland village of Warmenhuizen in 1846. We therefore consider it important to mention this earlier emigration with the names of the five heads of family: Jan Hendrik Wessels, Berend Hendrik Achteren, Johann Wilhelm Finder, Jan Berend Taalken, and Jan Berend Bruins.

This Roman Catholic emigration of 1845 may have been influenced from across the German border (Hanover).

1846 and 1847: Christian Secessionists

The Drenthe emigration to America of 1846-1847 gives a completely different picture: the emigrants from Drenthe are, without exception, Christian Secessionists.[8] This emigration from Drenthe was, in some ways, unique. Considering the country of the Netherlands as a whole, Dr. van Hinte summarizes:

> The Secessionists were not the only ones leaving the country (although their departure undoubtedly attracted the greatest attention), but also many *Nederlandsch-Hervormden*, more or less orthodox, many Roman Catholics, many "worldly" Netherlanders, some Mennonites, and a few *Zwijndrechtse Niewlichters*. The fact that of the 2331 heads of family who emigrated in the period between 1835 and 1848, only 653 stated that they were Secessionists and 449 stated that they were Roman Catholics, shows to what extent the number of Secessionists has been overestimated and that of the Roman Catholics underestimated.

It is regrettable that we cannot compare the figures from year to year. It is certain, however, that the 1846-1847 Trek from Drenthe consisted of one hundred percent of Christian Secessionists, which is very important in determining the character of the related schism in the villages of Drenthe.

This brings us to the motives advanced by the departing emigrants (or, rather, the motives ascribed to them). There were thirteen with religious motives, an equal number with economic motives, and forty-seven with a combination of the two. The reason formulated in Odoorn was remarkable: "They left, they said, to find a better living elsewhere; but actually because they believed that they would have greater religious freedom in America, or actually, that their convictions would be predominant there.''

This is an example of the typical trait found in Drenthian people, which camouflages deeper spiritual considerations by material motives!

1846

In the year 1846, thirteen families and four bachelors, altogether fifty-six persons, departed. Aside from farmers and farmhands, we find among the heads of families a merchant, the widow of a blacksmith, a painter, a carpenter, two tailors, and a weaver. They left at the same time as the Reverend van Raalte; they left Rotterdam on October 2, 1846, and traveled with him on the *Southern*. They belonged to the group known in American church history as the ''Pilgrim Fathers of the Nineteenth Century.'' Among them were five of the seven pioneers—the vanguard—who undertook the historic expedition of February 9, 1847, with the intent to establish Holland, Michigan. The average age of the family heads and independent bachelors was thirty-nine. Among other motives listed we find: ''Poverty and fanaticism,'' ''longing for improvement of their living standard,'' and ''great enthusiasm and the desire for a better living.'' The latter referred to Jan Rabbers, whose special enthusiasm would indeed soon become obvious in Michigan.

1847

Forty-four families and fourteen single persons left in the year 1847. This time, in addition to farmers and farmhands, there were a tanner's laborer, several carpenters, some tailors, two bakers, a shoemaker, a painter, a dyer in blue, a peat cutter, a blacksmith, and a servant girl. When recorded, the departure was in March 1847. This time the average age was higher, forty-two years; some of them were seventy or older. Among the persons of approximately sixty years of age, there were several who played an important part in the founding of the new colony; for example, Hendrik Lanning of Sleen (56), Jan Riddering of Sleen (59) and Jannes Weggemans of Sleen (64). For most, the destination was Michigan; only the people of Rolde listed Wisconsin. The motives were: ''According to their statements, the heavy taxes,'' ''poverty and fanaticism,'' or only the last reason (Hendrik Hunderman of Coevorden), ''exaggerated notions of freedom of religion and imagined hope of wealth and happiness without much work. This last reason was perhaps the strongest. . . .''

Financial Status

The one thing left is to give a summary of the requested financial status of the emigrants. The official report of the Provincial Government in 1848 states three distinct classes: prosperous, less prosperous, and poor. If we compare the individual statements of the various municipalities, we find that the meaning of ''less prosperous'' was interpreted in various ways. Sometimes a person who was ''rather well-off'' is listed in this category; sometimes one ''below the average''; another time a person who was ''reasonably well-off'' and had ''a good living as a farmer.'' Taking everything into consideration, I conclude that this ''less prosperous'' class had, through their wages, a reasonable livelihood, although they had little or no property at all. Of the sixty-seven registered persons, mostly family heads, there were forty-five considered less prosperous, fifteen poor, and seven prosperous. The van Raalte emigrants were generally considered to be ''people of little means'' when compared to the followers of the Reverend Scholte in Pella, Iowa. However, the Drenthe followers of the Reverend van Raalte definitely depart from the pattern. With a ratio of the three classes (prosperous, less prosperous, poor) being 7, 45, and 15, we probably come closer to a true cross section of the rural population of Drenthe. In this regard, the following comment of a Zweeloo reporter is of interest: ''Here, the desire to leave the native country exists exclusively with the Secessionists. It is not limited to any specific class, but rather seems to be the result of a certain religious confession.''

The following heads of families were listed as prosperous:

1. Harm Jans Smit, Hoogeveen, farmer and peatworker, age 56; Class 5 of poll tax.
2. Jan Riddering, Sleen, farmer, age 59; Class 5 of poll tax. (Estimated capital: fl. 11,000.)

3. Jannes Weggemans, Sleen, farmer, age 64; Class 8 of poll tax.
   (Capital: fl. 4,000.)
4. Hendrik Lanning, Sleen, farmer, age 56; Class 4 of poll tax.
5. Jan Zwiers, Westerbork, farmer, age 37; Class 13 of poll tax.
6. Jacob Nijenhuis, Westerbork, farmer, age 58; Class 8.
7. Jan Euving, Zweeloo, farmer, age 36; Class 8.

Apparently the poll tax refers to income, since I also found it under the category "less prosperous":

Class 2: 1	Class 10: 2
Class 3: 3	Class 11: 2
Class 4: 2	Class 12: 1
Class 5: 1	Class 13: 1
Class 6: 1	Class 14: 4
Class 7: 2	Class 16: 1
Class 8: 1	Class 17: 1

There also were twenty-seven nonassessed persons, and in Coevorden there was no poll tax at all.

So much for the confidential reports to the Governor of Drenthe and, through him, to The Hague. They have been of considerable use to us in determining the character of the Drenthe emigration around 1847. We can conclude from these reports that it shows a vertical economic structure, deviating from the general picture in Michigan. We will take this matter up again when we discuss the schism in the Drenthe rural community.

Later Emigration

The emigration to America continued in the years to come, but to a lesser degree. Dr. van Hinte provides the figures for the Netherlands in his standard work. Drenthe apparently had high and low figures similar to the rest of the country. The high point of the emigration was caused by the severe agricultural crisis of the Eighties. Again we find among the emigrants of this time many Reformed schismatics, for whom the road to America was more or less paved by their relatives and people of like mind who had left before them.[9]

But it was not only the Secessionists in Drenthe who were interested in emigration. Dr. H. Hartogh Heys van Zouteveen, of Assen, promoted emigration to California in the 1870s. And a few years later we find people from Drenthe active in South Dakota. Dr. van

Hinte writes: "Although the Dutch lived mainly among pioneers of other nationalities, a real purely Dutch settlement developed in the most northern border districts of Charles Mix and Douglas. A former peat cutter from the Dutch province of Drenthe, a Mr. A. Kuiper, Sr., who considered himself called by God for this task, especially acted as a leader."[10]

Through continued research one could gather more information about emigration from Drenthe during the second half of the century, with its improved mobility.[11]

[. . .]

Conclusion

In sum, one cannot but conclude that the people of Drenthe are not emigrants by nature. If there was any noteworthy emigration, it was during the turbulent years described by Dr. John Picardt, and it was motivated by a desire for self-preservation and preservation of one's possessions. Before that time and after, the primary reasons were economic. It is striking that if the villager of Drenthe chooses more fertile ground or better opportunities outside his old region, then he often obtains greater prosperity very quickly. Since he is used to working hard for a meager existence on poor land, he advances more rapidly with an equal amount of effort under more favorable conditions. Could it be that this was the reason that van Raalte made the choice for his vanguard primarily from these people?

The van Raalte Trek of 1847 is the more remarkable for Drenthe, because here primarily religious motives led to a breaking of the bonds of the village community. In this regard this emigration differs from other migrations of some magnitude. The Michigan Trek, therefore, deserves our special attention.

NOTES

1. See an article by Dr. J. Naarding in the monthly *Drente*, August 1947.

2. *"Jaarboekje voor Geschiedenis, Taal en Oudheidkunde der provincie* Groningen in *Groningsche Almanak*, 1910 (Groningen, Erven B. van der Kamp). Professor P. J. Blik had already published an article in the 1898 edition of the *Almanak*, "De herkomst van den Groninger stadsadel."

3. *Werken van den Ommelander Edelman Johan Rengers van ten Post;* editor, Mr. H. O. Feith. 1852, Vol. I, pp. 71, 72.

4. Professor Huizinga writes *Nederwolde,* but that should be *Roderwolde.*

5. "Beiler Zeevaarder uit de tijd der Republiek," in *Almanak,* under "Drente," XV, 8.

6. Governor and Representative of the King in Drenthe from 1846 to 1866.

7. Letter of December 21, 1847, No. 100, 6th section.

8. At that time the name *Christelijk Afgescheiden* was used more than *Gereformeerd.* Of the seventy-six emigrants reported, seventy were called *Christelijk Afgescheiden* and six *Gereformeerd.*

9. Concerning the emigrants from Beilen in 1889, see my article "Meer Drentsch-Amerikaansch Nieuws" in the *Nieuwe Drentsche Courant,* March 6, 1947.

10. Vol. II, p. 110.

11. Van Hinte tells about colonists in Colorado, originally from Noord Holland, Zeeland, Drente, Overijssel, Friesland, Groningen, Gelderland, and Noord Brabant. As the Reverend Bode wrote in *De Wachter:* "They go to church wearing gold headbands and gold temple-ornaments." Van Hinte, Vol. II, p. 233.

Interior of the Sleen church where Domine Van Raalte prepared his followers for the trek to America.

II

The Secessionists in Drenthe

THE DRENTHIAN AS SECTARIAN
FROM A SOCIOLOGICAL PERSPECTIVE

"Watchmen, what of the night?"
(Is. da Costa, 1847)

Soon after the liberation from Napoleonic France, religious tensions could be noticed in Drenthe between the men of the Enlightenment and the "objectors to the spirit of the age" (Da Costa, 1823). This tension was by no means due primarily to outside influences. Since 1825 or 1826, for example, secret worship meetings (conventicles) were organized by the Secessionists at the home of Frederik Kok, a shopkeeper, who later was a supporter of the Reverend H. de Cock of Ulrum (the "Father of the Secession"). Later Kok became the minister of the Reformed *(Gereformeerde Gemeente)* congregation in Dwingeloo.[1] These meetings were also conducted by Frederik's brother, Wolter, a farmer at the "Vossard" (about an hour's walk from Eemster in Drenthe). Later he was known as the Secessionist minister W. A. Kok of Ruinerwold (1842), became professor of the first theological school of the Secessionists, and also served several times as President of the General Synod.

The beginning of this theological training can be traced back to Dwingeloo, at the home of F. S. Kok. For some time the "school" was located in Groningen, when the Reverend de Cock was minister there, and later primarily in Ruinerwold at the Reverend W. A. Kok's home in de Bergen ("In the Mountains"). It was finally located partly in Hoogeveen, after the Reverend W. A. Kok had accepted a call there, and partly in Ulsen (Bentheim) at the home of the Reverend Bavinck, who was a pupil of the Reverend W. A. Kok. (Bavinck had been born in Bentheim and later served there as a pastor.) All these "schools" were forerunners of the Theological School of Kampen.

The two Kok brothers were the sons of the well-known "Master Albert" Kok (born in 1760 in Diever), a farmer in Eemster, an assessor of Diever, and a member of the citizens' guard of Diever during the French occupation. Before his marriage, Albert Hilberts (Kok) had been a schoolteacher in Diever (from 1784 to 1792). His nomination was signed by thirty *eigenerfden* (freeholders) of Diever, and it was considered noteworthy "that among these signatures there are so many names of parents and family members of clergymen who served in Secessionist parishes. All of them were pupils at Master Albert's school."

The Reverend J. Kok refers to this early Secession sentiment in Drenthe in his book about Master Albert. He traces it back to the Reverend H. J. Folmer, who served the Reformed Church at Dwingeloo from 1759 to 1781.[2] "Although he had died, he continued to speak, because forty years after his death there remained in Dwingeloo a remnant who professed the fundamental truths, which were no longer proclaimed in the church."[3]

This latent tension came to a fierce outbreak around 1834, the year of the Secession. In the provincial capital, Assen, there was on the one side the learned Reverend Dr. G. Benthem Reddingius, who had served the Hervormde Kerk [the former State Church] for many years and was widely known for his synodical duties. He had been a member of the Royal Commission for the Organization of the Hervormde Kerk in 1816. He was also known for a respectable number of publications (some scholarly), two of which had been awarded a prize by The Hague Association for the Defense of the Christian Religion. In these publications he proved himself to be a typical example of the "enlightened" clergyman. He also promoted the idea of "Progress": among his sermons there is one advocating small-pox vaccination (1817). His *Historical Picture Bible for Children* was denounced as "a work of the devil" by F. A. Kok, who was at that time an elder of the "returning" *Gereformeerde Gemeente* of Dwingeloo.

Reddingius sharply attacked the Secessionists in 1833 in his *Letters on the Present Dissensions and Movements in the Hervormde Kerk.* He regards the Secessionists "with sincere pity" and regrets their "narrow-minded ideas." In one of these letters he writes:

> It has been suggested that the behavior of most of the Secessionists should not be ascribed to bad principles or to a desire to cause confusion, but rather to ignorance and lack of insight. It has also been suggested that they are generally guided by a few ringleaders, who possibly (God only knows how!) are connected with the Jesuits. But why do they speak so boldly, so decisively, even against preachers, compared with whom, intellectually, they appear to be only miserable bunglers.

Reddingius was also one of the "two wolves" against whom the Reverend de Cock directed his best known work, *Defense of the True Reformed Doctrine and of the True Reformed People, Disputed and Exposed by Two So-called Reformed Ministers, Or: The Sheepfold of Christ Attacked by Two Wolves and Defended by H. de Cock, Reformed Minister at Ulrum* (1833). This is the famous polemic against the pastors Brouwer and Reddingius, after which the suspension procedure against de Cock increased. De Cock denounced them as "those who with might and main are leading souls to eternal perdition, defamers of what they do not understand, wolves, thieves, murderers, Pharisees, hypocrites, perjureres." (Quoted from the excerpts published by the Synod.)[4]

On the other hand, there was in Drenthe the remarkable Luitsen Dijkstra, initially a peat worker in Smilde, and an early participant in a conventicle that presumably met near the Norgervaart from 1825 or 1826. Later Dijkstra was an "exhorter under the Cross" at Smilde, then an officially ordained pastor of the Secessionist Church at Steenwijk "whose preaching Groen van Prinsterer [a well-known Dutch politician] did not hesitate to hear when he was spending a vacation at his estate *De Bult* on the Steenwijkerberg" (Rev. G. Keizer). Mr. J. de Haan, secretary of the municipality of Smilde, showed me the correspondence book of Mayor Kymmell (an 1835 report to the Governor), in which Kymmell wrote: "L. Dijkstra, who is called a pastor, is a poor laborer, whose upbringing was neglected. His younger years and part of his adult years were characterized by profligacy and dissipation. Later on, however, he elevated himself as the leader of the so-called pious souls, probably motivated by laziness and poverty, and by his ability (for someone of his social status) to speak well.''

Dijkstra was a devoted supporter of the Reverend de Cock, and he played a special role in the genesis of the Secession. At the urging of de Cock, Dijkstra once opposed Professor Hofstede de Groot with his *Poems, Written at the Request of Mr. H. de Cock, after Reading a Certain False and Blasphemous Booklet Entitled: ''Whom Are We to Believe, Man or God?''* De Cock wrote on the title page: ''The mysteries of the Kingdom of Heaven are hidden from the wise and understanding, but are revealed unto babes.'' After de Cock's suspension in 1833, Dijkstra led the meeting, attended by de Cock, which was held at the house of the widow Koster on the Sunday morning before Christmas (while the moderator was preaching in Ulrum).

How intensely people in the area felt about the conflict in Ulrum is evident from what Dr. Keizer writes in his work *The Secession of 1834* under the title ''Agreement with the Action of de Cock'':

> A farmer from the province of Drenthe wrote on March 1, 1834, to de Cock and his wife that in their meeting at the end of December they felt a deep empathy with de Cock and that they had therefore sung the third and fourth stanzas of Psalm 118, ''for, dearly beloved, believe it freely, God supplies people who pray for you, as we were given to do in our meeting yesterday.'' A fellow leader from Hoogeveen, who had conducted meetings in Assen on Wednesday and in Smilde on Thursday and Friday, was eagerly awaited, to tell how de Cock was doing and about the situation in Assen. A week before he had read a letter written by de Cock to a friend and had learned that the brothers and sisters in North Brabant held meetings twice a week. He states further that the minister of the Hervormde Kerk at Smilde stood shouting in front of nearly empty pews, especially on Sunday evening, ''whereas they were privileged to have at times, about three or four hundred people attending the meetings.'' In addition he very nicely gives his opinion regarding some newly published booklets. He regards de Cock's reply to a friendly question (number one) as a proper reply; he is looking eagerly for answer number two. The *Public Protestation* of Van der Werp and L. Dyjkstra meets everyone's approval, so that for a few days they were sold

out at the bookseller's in Assen as well as in Groningen. His friend
from Hoogeveen was able to purchase only two copies and these
he intended to send to Rev. C. He considers the writing of Them-
men van Wierum simple but effective. He is surprised at Klok's sharp
insight. He is disappointed that *The Defense of the Secessionists* has
been written anonymously. This letter will be delivered personally
by a friend and he also requests a reply.

This letter thus contains remarkable proof that the people in
Drenthe sympathized with the church conflict of 1834. All these
"little blue books" (that is, pamphlets by anonymous writers) and
other pamphlets that were then published in many editions and
in great variety, must have found many readers, mainly among
the unsophisticated. (The simultaneous movement of the *Reveil*
spoke more to Dutch intellectuals.) The bookseller in Assen mentioned in the letter was C. van Gorcum, founder of the Van Gorcum
Publishing House. Van Gorcum himself had also published two
brochures, the first one initially as a "little blue book," that is,
anonymously. It was entitled *A Modest Question for Truth's Sake Put
to Prof. P. Hofstede de Groot, as a Necessary Result of His Publication
"Thoughts on the Charge Against the Ministers of the Hervormde Kerk."*
This publication was also widely read, and a second printing was
published the same year, which revealed that J. A. Smeedes and
R. J. Veeninga were the authors. (R. J. Veeninga was later provincial
correspondent of the Secessionists.) A second publication was also
written by them. Evidently the Hervormde congregation of Assen
was in turmoil. In Meppel we also hear about "deeply concerned
brothers." When de Cock passed through Assen on his way to the
King in 1834 to discuss and clarify his affairs personally, the
following incident occurred: "People had hardly heard about de
Cock being in town, when the pious people gathered together. Talk-
ing about the concerns of the Kingdom of God, they encouraged
each other, admonishing, praying, and blessing each other, they
parted again."

Four weeks after the Secession in Ulrum, the second congregation of Secessionists was formed at Smilde. Assen was the third
congregation.[5] Then, on a Sunday in November 1834, "Master
Albert" walked out of a church service in Dwingeloo, "followed
by the major part of the congregation." In April 1835, a meeting
was held in the city of Groningen, with representatives from

Dwingeloo, Smilde, Assen, and Hoogeveen. In May 1835, the Reverend de Cock came to live in Smilde, where Deacon H. Sikkens had offered him a house. From then on he was pastor of the two northern provinces, but especially of Drenthe, and of Smilde and Dwingeloo in particular.

On October 31, 1836, a congregation was also founded in Diever, which was safe from persecution because supervision was in the hands of Assessor Hilbert Kok, the youngest son of "Master Albert." Hilbert Kok was a farmer and grocer, an assessor of the municipality, and a member of the Provincial States.

In 1836 Deacon Sikkens of Smilde traveled to the King with a petition on behalf of the congregations in Groningen and Drenthe, to request freedom of religion. At that time the Secessionist congregations were stil persecuted by public authorities "on the basis of a French law, promulgated by Napoleon after annexation of the Netherlands, against the agitators in the nation, that no more than twenty people were allowed to assemble without government approval." The change of kings in 1840 [when William I was succeeded by William II] made religious freedom a possibility. In 1841 permission was obtained for Diever, and in the same year a Secessionist church was built there. In 1843 Elder Hummelen of Diever, a painter by profession, became pastor of the new congregation of Nijeveen. The two brothers, Frederik and Wolter Kok from Eemster, who became pastors at Dwingeloo and Ruinerwold and later at Hoogeveen, and the famous L. Dijkstra of Smilde ("Dominie Luzien") have already been mentioned.

An independent Christian school had already been clandestinely founded in Dwingeloo under the name of "catechism class." Such a school had been in existence in Smilde since 1834. One of the oldest Reformed monthlies originated in Drenthe, namely, *De Herdersstem (The Voice of the Shepherd)*.

The most militant Secessionists in Drenthe were found in the western part, in the triangle formed by Assen, Hoogeveen, and Meppel. But this does not mean that the cause of the Secessionists did not exist in the southeastern part, called the Zuidenveld. Here, however, there were no sensational pamphleteers; instead, Calvinism revived in the privacy of the conventicles. The "Podagrists," a trio of writers in Drenthe, inform us in their travel journal of 1843 that "the Secessionists have a meeting place in Meppen." People of the Zuidenveld can still tell us that assemblies were

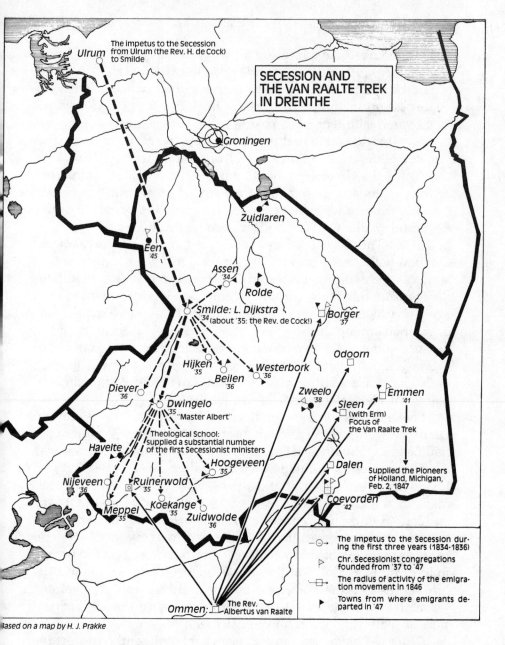

SECESSION AND THE VAN RAALTE TREK IN DRENTHE

The impetus to the Secession from Ulrum (the Rev. H. de Cock) to Smilde

Ulrum

Groningen

Zuidlaren

Een '45

Assen '34

Rolde

Smilde: L. Dijkstra '34 (about '35: the Rev. de Cock!)

Borger '37

Odoorn

Hijken '35

Westerbork '36

Beilen '36

Zweelo '38

Emmen '41

Diever '36

Dwingelo '35 "Master Albert"

Sleen (with Erm) Focus of the Van Raalte Trek

Theological School: supplied a substantial number of the first Secessionist ministers

Havelte

Hoogeveen '35

Dalen

Nijeveen '36

Ruinerwold '35

Supplied the Pioneers of Holland, Michigan, Feb. 2, 1847

Meppel '35

Koekange '35

Zuidwolde '36

Coevorden '42

—⊖—	The impetus to the Secession during the first three years (1834-1836)
▷	Chr. Secessionist congregations founded from '37 to '47
—□—	The radius of activity of the emigration movement in 1846
▶	Towns from where emigrants departed in '47

Ommen: The Rev. Albertus van Raalte

Based on a map by H. J. Prakke

held there, and that their parents or grandparents had been baptized in Meppen. There is an exaggerated yet pictorially excellent description of a village in Drenthe in those days by H. Tillema in *Folmers and His Contemporaries*. The story begins sometime in the 1820s, and the scene is at ''W,'' which probably is Wapse. In this story is described the grim struggle between the apostle of the progress of mankind and the exhorter of the conventicle.[6]

In the southeast of Drenthe another influence had its effect on the Secessionists during the forties—the influence of the Reverend A. C. van Raalte, who was pastor of the Secessionists at Ommen from 1840 to 1844. He had preached there even before that.[7] The Podagrists describe Ommen's central position in the province of Overijssel, the Graafschap Bentheim and the province of Drenthe, because of its annual fair, the *Ommerbissing*.[8] This center gained new importance for the Secessionists due to the presence of the Reverend van Raalte. The Podagrists note during another journey in 1843: ''The Secessionists also have a house of prayer here. Ommen will always play an important part in the history of this sect. We were told that a sort of academy has been founded here for its future ministers.''[9] In this connection it is important to read again what Dr. van Hinte writes in regard to the two streams that developed among the Secessionists: ''There is the northern or the de Cock–Joffers–Van Velzen party, consisting of people from Groningen, Friesland, and Drenthe, and the less conservative southern or Gelders party of Brummelkamp and Van Raalte, comprising the people of Gelderland and Overijssel.''[10]

I believe that the dividing line that van Hinte draws along the Drenthe-Overijssel provincial border should be drawn through the middle of the Province of Drenthe, since the southeastern part was strongly under the influence of van Raalte. One can see that van Raalte involved himself in the affairs of Drenthe by an advertisement in the *Drentsche Courant* of 1845. The advertisement was entitled ''Summons,'' and called the people to a day of fasting and prayer for the harvest. It was addressed to everyone ''who still believes that God blesses a nation or chastens it, so that the people may recognize Him,'' and it was signed by van Raalte and his brother-in-law, the Reverend H. Brummelkamp. This contact between van Raalte and Drenthe would prove fruitful later, in connection with the emigration to Michigan.

Thus we have seen how everywhere in Drenthe the people manifested themselves as ''sectarians.'' In sociological terms one can certainly call these early secessionist groups ''sects,'' as defined by Max Weber and adopted by Ernst Troeltsch. Out of protest they had freed themselves from the church into which they had been born or because of an inner unrest about the ecclesiastical uniformity [. . .].[11]

Such a remarkably courageous step was taken by many from Drenthe—people who, according to van der Kley, "do not like to separate themselves from the group. They therefore do not feel at home in foreign surroundings, far from their own village, and they prefer to join a new community as soon as possible. It often happens that people from Drenthe, from a village not dominated by a church, when they move to an orthodox community, adopt the prevailing opinions, faithfully attend church twice on Sunday, and send their children to a Christian school."[12]

Van der Kley and others are of the opinion that this "weakening of personality is caused by many centuries of cooperative activity in the collective village community." The people of Drenthe certainly are not born schismatics. The Trek of 1847 is therefore all the more interesting, because it is based, as we shall indicate later, on a sectarian attitude toward religion, and on the ecclesiastic circumstance in the villages.

NOTES

1. How the opposition viewed this can be read in the Rev. C. van Schaick's history of Dwingeloo, which Dr. Naarding brought to my attention. See van der Scheer's *Drenthsche Volksalmanak*, 1850, p. 10: "Meeting after meeting took place, especially at the home of Frederik Alberts Kok, store keeper and farmer, and later a Secessionist minister." Van Schaick is not very flattering in his account of this movement.

2. J. Kok, *Meister Albert en zijn Zonen. Uit de geschiedenis der Afscheiding in Drenthe* (reprinted in the Centennial year of the Secession [1934] by J. H. Kok, Kampen).

3. We shall never be able to succeed in determining completely the origin of any movement in human terms. For example, what was left of the spirit of the Nijkerk movement in southwestern Drenthe, which had made such inroads in 1750 that on November 10, 1751, the Synod of Drenthe felt called upon to interfere? See Dr. J. C. Kromsigt, *Wilhelmus Schortinghuis; Eene bladzijde uit de geschiedenis van het Pietisme in de Gereformeerde Kerk van Nederland* (Groningen: J. B. Wolters, 1904), p. 315.

4. See also Dr. Keizer, *The Secession of 1834*, p. 463.

5. See also Rev. B. Z. Bos, "Wat God heeft gedaan," in *De geschiedenis der Gereformeerde Kerk van Assen* (Assen: G. F. Hummelen, 1934).

6. H. Tillema, *Folmers en zijne tijdgenoten. Drentsche Novelle* (Kampen: K. van Hulst, 1868). This Folmers is no relation to the Reverend Folmers of Dwingeloo.

7. For an overview of the beginning of the Secession, see the pamphlet, *Gods Gunst Gedacht. 1836-1936*, prepared for the centennial of the Secession at Den

Ham near Ommen, by the Reverend J. H. Meuleman. This Secession, dated May 17, 1836, was led by the Reverend A. C. van Raalte, at the time not yet twenty-five years old. In 1837 van Raalte was called as pastor and preacher by the churches of Classis Ommen. He served these churches at first from Genemuiden. (After his ordination by the first Synod of the Secessionist church, early in March 1836, in Amsterdam, the Reverend van Raalte answered the call of the churches of Genemuiden and Mastenbroek on March 23, 1836.)

8. In *Een Drentsch Gemeente-Assessor met zijne Twee Neven op reis naar Amsterdam in 't voorjaar van 1843*, Part I (Groningen: C. M. van Bolhuis Hoitsema, 1845), p. 24.

9. To what extent these writers, as children of their time, belonged to the predominant faction is clearly evident from a passage in Part II of the *Assessor*, p. 385: ''He began to rebuke the cattle dealer earnestly for his shameful misuse of God's name in his daily talk and we soon discovered that he was one of those so-called students who are formed at Ommen under the direction of the so-called Rev. van Raalte, that is, trained, or drilled for the so-called ministry of the Secessionists!'' And they did not realize to what extent they further the latter's cause in a way they themselves regretted a little furthered on: ''We did not believe everything the angry man said, and we regretted that by uttering such untruths concerning the Secessionists he only fanned the fire of bitterness that already has caused a deep split between them and those of another persuasion.''

How low an opinion other important people had of the religious complaints of the Secessionists can be seen in this fragment of a lecture by the noted medical doctor from Hoogeveen, Dr. Michiel Dassen Hjzn: ''Only someone who lives in the midst of a farm community knows what exaggerated stories, what insignificant events lead to a decision to cross the ocean. At least for many who left for America from my area, the main reasons for their departure were exaggerated stories about the fertility of America, freedom of religion and education.'' *Over de doelmatigheid van het vestigen van Volksplantingen in warme gewesten* (Utrecht and Meppel: W. H. van Heyningen, 1849).

10. *Nederlanders in Amerika*, Vol. I, p. 391.

11. In their development, the Secessionist churches cannot be considered ''sects.'' ''The universality of their church organization and their Reformed church principles forbid this!'' (Prof. J. Lindeboon, ''Secte-wezen in Stad en Lande,'' *Groningsche Volksalmanak*, 1945.)

12. *Het Drentse Volkskarakter*, pp. 54-55.

III

Overpopulation and Emigration Fever Around 1847

SPECIFIC PROBLEMS IN DRENTHE

"Who will join us in going to the new Canaan?"
(From a cartoon ridiculing the emigration of the
Secessionists)

Overpopulation is a relative idea; it is actually a question of the possibilities for survival. Van der Scheer's *Drentsche Volksalmanak* of 1847 states: "It is only proper and wise that in a country such as ours, the most populated in the world, with a population of nearly 3,000,000, many are trying to emigrate elsewhere." A hundred years later, *Elsevier's Weekblad* (1947) writes: "Over-populated Netherlands, with 9,000,000 people! For several years now we can pride ourselves on having the greatest population density of all countries in Europe. A good international emigration plan is of primary importance."[1]

It is certainly true that the poor economic conditions of the 1840s in western Europe were the main reason for many to undertake the often dangerous journey to the distant wonderland of America. (The emigration fever came across our borders from Germany at Eibergen.) The difficulties encountered especially by our agrarian provinces were increased by the potato blight and the poor grain crop of 1845, providing additional motivation for seeking one's livelihood elsewhere—all of which point to economic reasons for the emigration of 1845-1847.[2]

However, it is also true that at least some of these emigrants were motivated by other, more spiritual, reasons. The leadership provided by the Secessionist preachers Brummelkamp, van Raalte, and later Scholte, was in the context of this spiritual motivation. When they discovered the possibility of America, they regarded this in the first place as a way to let their fellow believers escape from increasing unemployment and poverty; *but at the same time they wanted to avoid loneliness and dispersion, and therefore organized group colonization with an avowed Christian character.* (See van Hinte on this issue.) But, admittedly, the alleviation of economic need was of primary importance. In Arnhem, for example, where van Raalte lived at that time, provisions were made to enable the very poorest to emigrate with the others.

It may be helpful to compare the situation of the emigrants from Drenthe with the general situation in the Netherlands. When describing the condition of the laborers of that time, van Hinte puts Drenthe in a very unfavorable light: "Worst of all was the situation in the heather fields. . . , or in Drenthe, where the houses were little different from pigstys" (Vol. I, p. 87). (This is a false generalization that must be contested!)

The well-known Christian philanthropist, the Reverend O. G. Heldring, founder of the Heldring Institutions, published a pamphlet dedicated to his friend I. da Costa, entitled *Colonization at Home and Abroad in Relation to Poverty*,[3] which was well known in Drenthe, since van der Scheer had an article on it in the 1847 *Drenthsche Volksalmanak*. This pamphlet also provides us with contemporary information. Heldring was a noble person with keen insight. Among other things he mentions the possibility of reclamation of the Zuiderzee "for colonization and small-scale farming by reliable people." Heldring, together with the Reverend H. P. Scholte, also tried working together in the "Committee for the Secessionists and for Many Poor Countrymen" to interest the government in The Hague in promoting emigration to "our East-Indian Colonies." "Our arguments did not meet with much success—too little to encourage the Secessionists to seek their future in that direction." [. . .] If it had been successful, there might have been a Drenthe on Ceram or Buru, instead of a Drenthe in Michigan.

Heldring gives exact figures to show the economic distress of the workers: "During the winter a farmhand in Zuylichem

(Gelderland) threshed from dawn to sunset for a wage of one nickle (*stuiver*)." If he "digs heavy clay soil, he can earn six nickles a day. A farmhand in the Betuwe [the most fertile part of Gelderland] earns ten nickles for twelve hours of work."[4] [. . .]

But then comes the passage to which we must pay special attention.

> This spring when the news was published by the cautious *Staats-Courant* that there was sufficient work in the province of Drenthe, and that a daily wage of one and a half guilders could be earned, many people went there. But they returned poorer than ever. They said: "We cannot do this kind of work. We could not even earn our own living, much less for wife and children." People can't be transformed into peat workers just like that. That's a job for giants. Whoever wants to work there has to be accustomed to the hardest possible work. He has to be tough as leather, tireless, unusually healthy, and hardened. After paying for his Munster and Westphalian food, he can still save a good bit of money.

These words depict Drenthe (even officially) more like an economic El Dorado in those poor times, at least for the worker who was used to hard work.[5]

There are also some relevant statistical data, published by Dr. W. Steigenga in an article, "Remarks Pertaining to the Growth of Population in the Dutch Rural Districts."[6] In this article Steigenga compares figures between 1840 and 1880 in the provinces of Groningen, Friesland, Drenthe, and Zeeland in relation to agrarian issues. In one of his conclusions he points out the

> striking fact of sizable migration into Drenthe during the 1840's, which was probably the result of the increased cultivation of the heath. During this decade [and that is exactly the period that is of interest to us in regard to the Michigan Trek; Prakke] the population increase doubled as a result of the migration. Only after 1870 did a segment of the population increase in Drenthe have to move elsewhere, although until 1921 this emigration remained rather small.

The statistics are as follows:

I. *Increase or decrease of population during 1840-1850*

	Birth Surplus	Migration	Total
Groningen	9.22%	-1.94%	7.28%
Drenthe	6.64%	7.51%	14.15%

| Friesland | 9.66% | -1.10% | 8.56% |
| Zeeland | 7.58% | -1.68% | 5.90% |

II.   *Part of the increased population caused by growing birth rate that had to move elsewhere in the period of 1840-1850*

Groningen	21%
Drenthe	*-113%*
Friesland	12%
Zeeland	22%

It thus becomes clear that, from an economic point of view, Drenthe differed sharply from other agrarian provinces. In Drenthe around 1840, the motivation for emigration because of economic factors was much less compelling than in other agrarian provinces.

In earlier centuries the cultivation of new land in Drenthe had been undertaken by the population on a limited scale, only to suit their increasing needs. According to the *Grondschattingsregister* of Ruinerwold, my great-great-grandfather cleared no more than one *hectare* at a time. In the nineteenth century, however, cultivation on a larger scale would be undertaken by outsiders. In their book on Drenthe (1843), the Podagrists exclaimed as follows:

> How much soil remains unused, soil which could be wisely used for large gain, if only someone would tackle the problem forcefully. Drenthe will therefore be, for many more years, the province of development and progress, even when people in Holland and elsewhere will complain about stagnation and decay. As to the province of Drenthe, the Golden Age still has to blossom from the bud of time; it still is in its childhood—its youth still lies in the future. Canals and roads! That is the demand upon Drenthe's governors; it does have the same rights as the other provinces. No more provincialism in the nineteenth century![7]

Thus the economic situation in Drenthe was definitely less serious than elsewhere in our country. As to the standard of living of the working man, although it may have been far from ideal in many ways, van Hinte's description of the pigsty was unreasonable and not valid as a motivating factor for emigration. The people of Drenthe had always been forced to depend only on their own strength, because they were accustomed to the unproductive soil and to an inferior position compared to the other provinces ("the stepchild Drenthe"!). This is also confirmed by figures from a government report after the crop failure of 1817. The number of welfare recipients in the Netherlands had increased to eleven percent of the population, but in Drenthe it increased only to five percent.[8]

And it was with a selected group of these Drenthian people, trained in such an environment, that, on October 2, 1846, van Raalte embarked from Rotterdam on the *Southerner*, with the rather indefinite destination: "North America."[9]

NOTES

1. Dr. F. Bakker Schut, *Elsevier's Weekblad*, April 19, 1947. Hendrik Lanning and the many other pioneers in the building of Holland, Michigan, should be thankful that a century ago people were still free to roam God's world if they felt the urge to do so! Today, before such plans could materialize, they would have to be approved first by national and international programs. Many people now would be considered "too old" or called "unsuitable" psychologically, and certainly would be unable to take all their belongings with them to start anew.

2. It is interesting to consider the economic motivation which J. J. Uilenberg recalled in the *Provinciale Drentsche en Asser Courant*, February 18, 1948, in reaction to my series of articles in that newspaper: "At the time of the Drenthe exodus my father was a schoolboy in Erm. The Lannings emigrated from Erm. Without a doubt they were very well acquainted with my family, because in my youth Father sometimes read to us from an old yellowed letter from Lanning. One quote I have always remembered:

> Everyone here in this land
> eats the fruits of his own hand:
> only pure grain and no sand.

The writer then referred to a psalm, which we looked up, probably Psalm 128. Simple words, but of historical significance. Father must have given us an explanation something like this: In the Forties we had a tax on butchering and flour grinding. Not one bag of flour left the mill without the seal of the tax inspector. In order to avoid the tax, a poor farmer would say, "It is for the pigs." (Feed for cattle was tax free.) In order to make the flour really unfit for human consumption, the inspector would throw in some sand from a bag and mix it thoroughly. This mixture was then eaten, with teeth grinding, by the pigs—and by the poor farmers and workers. "There they eat sand," is still an expression from that time to indicate that a family was not very well off.

Lanning probably was not one of the "sand eaters" himself, but he must have been one of those who despised this practice of the government, and for this reason sought a new homeland." (In this article the writer tells that after World War I, he found a grave of the Drenthian-American H. R. Lanning in an American Army Cemetery in the French village of Roagne.)

3. Published in Amsterdam by G. J. A. Beyerinck (1846). This study was the result of a speech by Heldring at the Agricultural Planning Congress at Zwolle (1845?) concerning "Colonization Within our Country," and his consequent appointment to a commission for examining the possibilities of free colonization in the homeland. On the commission was a Drenthian, Mr. Thomkens (or Tonckens) from Westervelde. Drenthe had already been considered earlier for such projects by General van den Bosch and his "Organization of Social Welfare,"

to combat poverty after the French occupation. However, these colonies (Veenhuizen and Frederiksoord) became an expensive miscalculation and discredited the whole movement to colonize the moors, because poverty-stricken settlers were sent there, without regard to their ability or attitude toward working.

4. In this same article it is estimated that it cost 500 guilders to send a family to America to settle as colonists. For one person it cost 70 guilders.

5. Harm Drent, a favorite poet of Drenthe, whose interest in my study I appreciate very much, contested the idea of an Eldorado in a series of articles on the Reverend C. van Schaick (minister at Dwingeloo from 1838 to 1852 and thus a contemporary of our emigrants), and on the recession of 1800-1850 (*De Provinciale Drentsche en Asser Courant*, February 21 – April 17, 1948). Of course, I did not use the idea in an absolute but in a comparative sense. Was not my conclusion that the problems here were "less gloomy" than in other places in the country?

Nevertheless, Harm Drent continues to insist "that it was mainly material considerations that made the Secessionists decide to go to America." He bases this judgment partly on an article by the Reverend van Schaick in *De Nederlandsche Volksbode* of 1848, entitled "Landverhuizens en landverhuizing," a "well-founded thesis" that characterizes the question of emigration correctly "in spite of a certain prejudice" (van Schaick's antipathy to the group of the Reverend de Cock). "Religious freedom cannot be a motive, according to him. All who want permission from the king to found a church, to form a congregation, and to support a minister out of their own pockets can receive such permission if they only submit their constitution and creed. No group has yet been refused. No one is making it difficult for you here." Yes, to some degree the situation in 1848 could be viewed this way, if the lack of freedom and the "bother" (euphemistically speaking) of the recent past were overlooked. And van Schaick undoubtedly was sincere when he admonished, "Be careful what you are doing!" after seeing three ships at the Diever bridge with emigrants from lowly Drenthe on their way to America—but this does not show much sympathy for the feelings of people of a different persuasion. And it shows no understanding whatsoever of the depth of the wounds inflicted so recently. In many villages they never healed completely.

6. *Tijdschrift voor Economische Geographie*, XXXIV, No. 8, Aug. 15, 1943.

7. *Drenthe in Vlugtige en Losse Omtrekken geschetst*, by Drie Prodagristen (D. H. van der Sheer, H. Boom, and A. L. Lesturgeon) I (Koevorden: D. H. van der Scheer, 1843). See also *Het Boek der Podagristen* by Dr. J. Naarding, Dr. P. W. J. van den Berg, Professor A. E. van Giffen, with an introduction by H. J. Prakke and Dr. R. D. Mulder (Assen: Van Gorcum and Co., 1947).

8. See Dr. H. T. Colenbrander, *Willem I*, Vol. II, p. 157. The Central Bureau for Statistics informed me that these data do appear in the *Handelingen der Staten Generaal of 1817*. From a report concerning poverty in the Netherlands of 1817, the Central Bureau was so kind to add the following list of percentages of the population receiving financial assistance from the government:

Groningen	5.1%
Friesland	8.3%
Drenthe	4.7%
Overijssel	5.6%
Gelderland	7.1%
Utrecht	9.3%
Noord-Holland	21.9%

Zuid-Holland	11.2%
Zeeland	8.0%
Noord-Brabant	10.1%

9. See the list of passengers of the *Southerner*, Appendix II.

The majestic tower of the Sleen church was built between 1420–1450. The church itself dates back to 1338.

IV

The People of Sleen

EMIGRATION UNDER THE MICROSCOPE

"Even Menso Alting's voice found no
response here: Sleen banished him"
(T. J. *Servatius in* Album Amicorum;
Dr. J. *Naarding, 16-6-1947*)

The municipality of Sleen supplied most of the emigrants for the
Michigan Trek of 1846-1847, especially the village of Erm, which
is a part of Sleen. Sleen and Erm are both farming communities
of medieval origin. The oldest charter of Sleen dates from 1160,
and that of Erm from 1302. Of the total population of Sleen, five
percent left for Michigan; of Erm, ten percent. Is there anything
in the history of this community that can lead to a better understanding of the conduct of these villages around 1847?

To my knowledge Sleen never enjoyed a special reputation for
piety, even though a church was established there at an early date
with a very old bell (cast in 1400), which was dedicated to the Virgin
Mary. Moreover, the ancient Mary-plays demonstrate that, in those
days, such devotion to her could compensate for much neglect of
religious duties.

If the people of Sleen were not exactly model Catholics in
medieval times, they did not differ much from other inhabitants
of Drenthe. In fact, from ancient times Drenthe had the reputation
of being only semichristianized. Emperor Charlemagne converted
the Saxons to Christianity by the sword, and nowhere does one

see so many remaining pagan morals and customs, as, for example, the Easter bonfires.[1] As a rule church involvement is not typical for such a medieval agricultural society.

In Drenthe there were hardly any monasteries with their beneficial influence. There were a few in the north (Assen) and in the southwest (Ruinen-Dikninge), but their influence would hardly be evident in the southeast where Sleen is the principal city. There was some contact with Assen, however. In a document of 1484, Wilm ten Holte (representing his cousin Gierd Hubbeldinge) declared that the people of Sleen had donated a farm to the monastery of Assen.[2] The *Podagrists* write that this monastery also had some properties at Erm. More important for us is the information from the same source that in those days Erm was part of Emmen. ''Even today [1840s] the minister of Emmen draws a rent in kind, a small share of the rye harvest, called 'Maundy Thursday rye,' from the hamlet of Erm. This is collected in very small quantities. This contribution supposedly entitles the people of Erm to the use of a path leading to Emmen, which has to be wide enough for two women wearing hoop-skirts to pass each other without hindrance.'' Even today there is a direct connection between Erm and Emmen.

In Emmen the emigration started in 1846, as it did in Coevorden, which is situated on the road from Emmen to Erm and Ommen. From Emmen came Jan Rabbers and the pioneers Egbert Vreriks and Evert Zagers; from Noordbarge, Willem Kremers (as his son Henry Kremers informed me); from Erm, K. Hunderman, H. Stokking, Hendrik Lanning, Klaas Schoemakers, G. J. Hunderman (according to their auction advertisements in the *Drentsche Courant*), and also the farmers Jan Jalving, Gerrit Ratering, and Jan Strabbing (for whom I could not locate auction notices) and perhaps some others.[3] The old church-path may have promoted contact between persons with a similar interest.

But I was searching for special spiritual motivations! When the Reformation reached Drenthe, Sleen had the privilege of being the first parish where the new doctrine was preached. This was performed by Menso Alting, an alumnus of the Heidelberg School. But he did not find any listeners. It is said that he was nearly stoned to death by the people and had to flee for his life. In 1567 he left Drenthe and went to the Paltz in Germany. Later on (May 10, 1598), the Reformation was introduced in Drenthe by a decree of Stad-houder Willem Lodewijk. Thus, christianized by the sword and reformed by the decree of a stadhouder!

In *Het Kerkkrantje* of Odoorn, Dr. Naarding has just developed an interesting theory, which departs radically from the generally accepted one.

> The official documents provide little information concerning the Reformation in Drenthe. The vehement reaction of the people of Sleen to the modern ideas of Menso Alting has already been referred to and is gladly quoted, especially in Catholic quarters, as proof of faithfulness to the Mother Church of Rome. But one can just as well find a denial of faithfulness in the fact that prohibited open-air ser-vices must have been held there regularly; these were held near the burial stones (*hunebed*) on the road to Schoonoord, which ever since has been called "the popeless church." Could it be that the passion-ate Calvinist Menso Alting clashed in Sleen with the older Lutheranism which was of a different nature? Then the opposition would not be proof of faithfulness to Rome, but of a rejection of Calvinism, with its severe consequences; this Calvinism is incom-patible with the Drenthian character, as it still has not been able to conquer the old Drenthian communities in the sandy regions. My supposition that Sleen, and all of Drenthe, was already considerably won over to Lutheranism before Calvinism was preached there finds support in the chronicles of Picardt, who says that around 1530 many lay people and even clergy had joined the Reformation (that is, Luther). These chronicles agree with the wording of a request from the same period by the abbey of Assen to the high bailiff of Drenthe, which complains about "Lutheran heresies," which have caused the oppression and humiliation of "all clergymen." And thirty years later, in 1560, the abbot of the Groningen monastery in Aduard, who had supervision of the nunnery in Assen, writes to his chief, the bishop of Munster, that the nuns are in dire need, since the popula-tion in Drenthe is strongly polluted with all kinds of heresies and hence neglects the church and its institutions.[4]

Naarding's hypothesis makes one wish that more historical research were done in our province.[5] After spending one Saturday afternoon rummaging through a chest of church archives in the hospitable parsonage of the Reformed Church at Sleen, I realized that an ocean of research is awaiting any serious person interested in church history.

Whatever the merit of Naarding's hypothesis, even after the official Reformation of 1590 there was no evidence of exaggerated religious zeal. Sixteen parishes obtained a clergyman in 1598, but Sleen, the main town of the district, received its first Protestant pastor only in 1600. The pastor was Hermannus Alers Swollensis who, according to earlier church records, was not altogether spotless; he also served and remained in Sleen until 1615. He had been a Catholic vicar at Diever and after the Reformation he was retained (like some other priests) as a minister on the condition that he had to be examined "in the principal articles of the Christian faith." When the highest church assembly in Drenthe met at Rolde on June 9, 1600, Alers had not yet passed the examination.[6] The last "papist" (Catholic priest) of Sleen was Johannes Steenbach; after the Reformation on May 10, 1599, his name is not mentioned anymore. The Stadhouder had given instructions that these papists had to leave their parsonages and declare on oath that they would keep silent, not conduct any divine service, nor stir up anyone secretly or publicly. In Sleen, however, people seemed to prefer the old ways. The new provincial church authorities had no prestige, as they themselves admitted (*Acta* of December 9, 1600). In 1602 there was again "doubt about the minister" (*de pastore dubitatur*). In 1603 it was worse still: Herman Alers was charged with manslaughter at Diever. At the Classis General it was said that he acted in self-defense. Nevertheless, the Classis was of the opinion that the minister could not continue in office. The attitude of the people of Sleen after Alers' "accident" was remarkable:[7] they declared that most people of Sleen rather liked him! Apparently they were not zealots. And their forebearance won. At the next Classis General their minister attended again as usual; the Classis, however, resolved to refer the problem to the University of Franeker in Friesland. Four years later the case remained unfinished, because of costs.

In 1608 the Reformed Church called a meeting in Assen of all the parishes in the Classis of Drenthe, in order to examine the state of the church properties and the situation of the parishes and ministers. All the parishes in Classis Emmen sent rather large delegations, but behind the name of Sleen appears the notice: "Mayor and church-wardens absent." Again, no indication of lively interest![8] Pastor Alers was there alone and declared himself satisfied with his parish, with the people diligent in church attendance. The same meeting then dismissed the manslaughter charges and appointed Alers permanently to ministerial service in the district.

In 1675 Pastor Alers, who the year before had been excused from the Classis General because of old age and infirmity, was replaced by a rather different person: Henricus Huysinck. The September 5, 1615 Acts of the Classis General in Assen record: ''That he had graduated with honors from the Academy of Franeker and had passed the examination of the Classis. He had been admitted as minister of Sleen by the provincial Synod after he had signed the Netherlands Confession and the seventeen additional articles.''

Husingius (Huysinck) appears to have been a Calvinistic heresy hunter. At the September 1618 Synod in Assen he charged his colleague Johannes Rusius with Arminianism. Sleen, at the time that Husingius arrived, had already experienced seventeen years of official ''Reformation.'' With Alers' leadership serving as shock absorber, it had not been a fierce beginning. Sleen had already accepted its new status under the changed circumstances when the far more passionate Husingius appeared.

Ministers came and left. In Sleen fanatics and nonfanatics, extremists and moderates must have succeeded one another. On the whole, men of tolerance gained ground during the eighteenth century. When de Cock and his followers sounded the alarm, Enlightenment and Progress were the dominating ideas in the State Church. It is not surprising that Sleen was no exception to the general state of affairs.

When the Podagrists made their journey through Drenthe in 1843, the pastor at Sleen was the Reverend Otto Schultz, born in the neighboring German town of Graafschap Bentheim. Although this trio always observe keenly and are attentive to church affairs [. . .], yet in the detailed description of Sleen there is no indication whatsoever that could point to the amazing fact that nearly three years later a wave of schismatic emigration should erupt from this community. It seemed to be all peace and quite there.

''Now we come to Sleen . . . . Do you want a clear picture? Then imagine a small village such as we tried to sketch in Westerbork, but built in a less orderly fashion, without anything looking like a street, and yet with about fifty houses, trees, gardens, walls, pastures, sheepfolds, wagon sheds and the usual accoutrements of a village in Drenthe. *And what about the way of life? Exactly the same as elsewhere.* That is to say, that the farmer here rises early or late, according to the time of the year . . . ," and so forth. The Podagrists also visited the church; they mention the old bells and the heavy stone baptismal font (now in the Museum in Assen), and comment on the pulpit "as naked and unpainted as it stands there with its sounding board, it is nevertheless decorated with a couple of biblical texts."[9] The whole impression is rather poor: "With so much that is of no importance, we may not fail to record . . . ," and then follows the story of Menso Alting. In addition, they mention all the ministers who served there. Schultz appears to have been there since 1840.

Was this the calm before the storm? On the secular plane Sleen had already known disturbances in the period of the anti-Orange patriots (*Keezen*) before the French Revolution. Indeed, Sleen had a certain importance in worldly affairs as the principal town of the district of Zuidenveld, so that one may assume that politicians with a wider political interest lived there. Those disturbances in the eighteenth century found expression at that time in a *Keezen-Societeit* at Sleen, a patriotic club called "Training School for Rights and Privileges." Their records had been discovered, but are now unfortunately lost again. Dr. Linthorst Homan, who cited the 1787 records in his dissertation, comments: "Indefinite wishes. The articles clearly demonstrate the vagueness. Likewise the great influence of defamation—not unusual in such times."[10] How I would have liked to check these records, especially to research family names of opponents, to determine if the old antagonisms played a role in the emigration and schism, since religious and secular issues were at that time closely interwoven. And family feuds in Drenthe are of a persistent nature, not only flaring up during the fair or the yearly market. Such feuding does not, of course, detract anything from the deeper motives. But it does quite often determine close relationships and well-known divisions in the village community.

The Reverend Otto Schultz began his duties at Sleen with much enthusiasm, as is evident from the nicely leather-bound register

of sermons that his grandson and granddaughter showed me when
I visited them one afternoon on their farm at Erm: "Records of texts
and various subjects on which I preached, with the year they were
preached. First the regular sermons are listed; next, sermons for
special occasions, such as New Year's, New Year's Eve, a prayer
day, preparation for communion, etc." Some titles for special
occasions read as follows: the battle of Waterloo, "Justice elevates
a people"; and on vaccination, "Behold, children are a heritage
of the Lord." The record reveals that the Reverend Schultz belonged
to the "enlightened" group of preachers, and must have advocated
general, though vague, liberal ideas.

This liberalism *did not, however, wholly define his place in the
community of Sleen and especially not in Erm,* and eventually it was
not even of prime importance. His marriage to a rich farmer's
daughter of Achterste Erm thrust him into the midst of the family
problems in a Drenthian village, which appeared unified from the
outside, but from the inside . . . . The Abbings were a family of
substance; a part of Achterste Erm still bears the name of *Abbinger-
end.* But in Achterste Erm lived another farmer of no less substance,
Hendrik Lanning, who in the *Drentsche Courant* of March 12, 1847,
announced a public sale of "a complete farming estate consisting
of 2 horses, 20 cows, 50 sheep, hay, straw, furniture, etc." On
March 26 there was a second auction of "a farm, 7½ hectares of
cultivated land, an 18 work-days hayfield, 12 cow pastures and a
3/8 *waarwaardeel* share in the undivided *Markte* of Erm. . . , because
of departure to North America." In a secret report to the Governor
of the Province his wealth was estimated at fl. 16,000, which was
a large amount for Drenthe in those times.

In the same way K. Hunderman sold a well-furnished farmhouse, with hay and pasture fields, located in Erm, as well as one-
fourth of a *waarwaardeel* in the *Markte* of Erm; H. Stokking, a
blacksmith at Erm, auctioned off a considerable number of tools,
12 cows, 20 sheep, farmer's implements, and furniture; and Klaas
Schoemaker sold a farmhouse with farm, hay and pasture fields,
and a *waarwaardeel,* all located in Erm. The same procedure was
followed in Noord Sleen by a man of substance, Jan Riddering,
and in Zuid Sleen by his associate Johannes Weggemans. The
reason for all these auctions: "Because of departure to North
America"—reflecting the denouement of a dramatic tension of long
standing in the village community.

But this was not yet the end of the tension. On May 30, 1848, the Reverend O. Schultz was provisionally suspended by the church authorities in order for a committee to investigate the matter. And on June 15: "A committee is appointed in the very sensational case of O. Schultz, minister at Sleen, to investigate an attempted suicide as well as other shocking rumors circulated about said person." Then follow all sorts of distasteful accusations. Many witnesses are summoned: the church board, the schoolteacher, the neighbors, the servants who lived with the minister at the time, the catechism teacher, the physician Dinckgreve, and some others, known by the board as having frequently visited the house of the minister; and at last the minister himself was heard. The testimony was unanimous: that they indeed had heard the rumors, but that they had never seen the minister drunk or unable to function; they had never noticed any quarrels at home, not even those who were at the parsonage on a daily or frequent basis. The attempted suicide was ascribed to temporary insanity, which was confirmed by the written testimony of two different physicians. It was decided to lift the suspension, but a recommendation was made to the consistory of Sleen to keep their clergyman under special supervision.

How sharp accusations about people's conduct were, also from those opposed to the Separatist movement, can be seen from a jingle circulated in Sleen of which we quote eight lines:

> He is even a secessionist,
> But his fate is miserable.
> He does not serve the Lord—
> The devil is his God.
> Do you also want to secede?
> Do so with careful thought—
> Separate from evil
> And walk in the ways of God.

We can feel the tension that must have been present in this village community during the years before the crisis came. The whole network of old feuds, slander, and backbiting must have been operating. But it would be wrong to reduce the whole event to this feuding. Back of it all was the tension between the two ecclesiastical parties; or rather, this tension was at the root of it all.

It was worthwhile to examine the "Records of the Acts of the

Handbill lampooning the intentions and experiences of the religious
emigrants bound for the New Land.
A contemporary satire of Van Raalte's Followers.

"Who wants to come with us
to the New Canaan?"

1.

"O Father Unrest! To that promised
land we feel a strange attraction!"

2.

"We have walked down these
'Greenlandish' alleys so often!"

3.

"America! The land of our desires!"

4.

A farmer and his wife, 75 years old,
leaving for America
to die—just for a change.

5.

A scene on board ship.

6.

Spiritual union.

7.

Colonization through population.

8.

Arrival.   *Disembarkation.*

1.   2.

Division by lot.   *Setting fire to prairie grass.*

3.   4.

While the husband works the land,
a lion devours his wife
and an eagle steals his child.   *Bram under the fig tree.*

5.   6.

Spiritual confusion in speech
and languages.   *The fall of the colony.*

7.   8.

» Jij, je bint een na-   » Ik heb den   » Arme BRAM ! "   » Blief je wat te geven,
tuurlijk mensch, naakt   geest ! "   of doe je het niet graag?"
en blind ! "

Consistory at Sleen.'' There I found the minutes kept by Schultz since 1840 in what seemed to be a short annual report:

1840/42: Nothing.

1843: The regrettable Secession of some members did not increase this year but appears to be declining.

1844: We may rejoice at the ever increasing religious consciousness in the congregation. The Secession did not make any gains.

1845: The religious conviction and situation in the congregation is as it was last year.

1846: The regrettable Secession languishes more and more. Many of the Secessionists are selling their properties in order to emigrate to North America.

1847: The religious attitude is the same as last year.

1848: An extraordinary church investigation has taken place on account of the illness of the minister and the condition of the congregation, which turned out to the satisfaction of the congregation. The faithful attendance of the members at church services testified to the increasing affection for religion.

1849/50: Nothing.

1851: The regrettable Secession is diminishing.

A few days or perhaps a few weeks after Schultz had written this last entry he again attempted suicide—and this time he succeeded. The next minutes are written by the moderator of neighboring Oosterhesselen, the Reverend A. L. Lesturgeon (the youngest of the three Podagrists).

The Secession had pierced Schultz's soul. Till the end he had fought for unity as he saw it. ''Oh, Rev. Schultz was terribly hostile towards the Secessionists, Father Wilting told us many times,'' said the widow of the late H. R. Lanning of Noord Sleen when I visited her a few months ago. She still had in her possession a letter, written in Michigan in 1847 by the emigrant Hendrik Lanning to her husband's grandfather, Remmelt Lanning, in Noord Sleen: ''As far as we are concerned, we don't wish ever again to set foot on Dutch soil. You probably ask why that is. I rejoice in meeting God's people here. They don't blaspheme God's name. But, when I was still living in the Netherlands, the servants of Satan reigned. . . .''

As Mrs. Lanning told me, it was not until 1877 that Sleen had a Secessionist Reformed Church. Previously they attended church in Emmen. And even earlier they had held services in a house in Meppen; her mother had been baptized there in one of the rooms. Erm, and especially Achterste Erm, have, comparatively, the most Secessionist people, but they are a minority everywhere, and there are still many sensitive issues.

These sensitivities manifested themselves likewise in Sleen when the Reverend M. Beversluis founded an Orthodox-Hervormd "Evangelization" in the 1880s. It is characteristic, however, that it was not called "Evangelization," but simply a "Hall" for church-related activities. In the beginning the Drenthian sense of unity also prevailed with the followers of the Reverend Beversluis. There was no intention of opposing the official religion. In this struggle between the great majority who were in favor of unity and a minority in favor of purity of doctrine, we come across the same family names in a later generation—again opposed to each other. In Sleen it was said of the Reverend Beversluis that his preaching was too profound.

In summary, I must conclude that throughout the ages the community spirit of Sleen (and of Erm) was characterized by a strong aversion to any infringement on the unified life-style. In ecclesiastical matters the people also clothed their personal religious conviction in the garb of village collectivity as long as possible. The tension must have been very strong indeed for the people to have broken with this attitude. And the tension apparently did become too strong for Hendrik Lanning and his associates. The French occupation and the conditions that preceded and followed the occupation had weakened the authority of the traditional village leaders. The church was less central than before: church pronouncements had disappeared,[11] and civil weddings had virtually replaced church weddings. And church officers, including the Reverend Schultz, not only accepted this development, but even welcomed it as Progress and Enlightenment. [. . .]

The moment came when even solid members of the *Marke* in Sleen, such as Hendrik Lanning, became so alarmed in their conscience about the course of events in politics and especially in the church under the Reverend Schultz that they no longer conformed to the Drenthian stereotype. In discussions of these matters with the minister and his supporters they no longer resorted to the usual answer: "It must be as you say, Reverend," but, according to a characteristic story by Anne de Vries, they blew their tops, pounded with their fists on the table, and shouted, "I don't believe a word of it, Reverend!"[12]

Without anticipating in any way what I would find, or even if I would find anything of importance for my research there, I went for a close look to Sleen and Erm, the focal points of the emigration schism of 1846-1847. The results far surpassed my expectations. Fragments, found here and there, fell into place and revealed a dramatic occurrence of great tension: the first schism in an old village community in Drenthe.

NOTES

1. See, for example, Dr. P. W. J. van den Berg, "Kerk en Volksleven" in Poortman, *Handboek Drente*, Vol. I, pp. 290-291, 294.

2. Inventory Abbey, Assen. Register No. 99.

3. For this information I am indebted to Mr. G. A. Bontekoe for his search of the Archives. The information again shows very clearly that it was a true cross-section of the community, real "Drenthians," and not a motley group of newcomers from somewhere else, which separated from the community: well-to-do farmers, poor farmers, farm laborers, and various tradesmen. Only a few times do we find those with an origin from somewhere outside of Drenthe, normally from neighboring Bentheim.

4. This *Kerkkrantje* of the Reverend H. van Lunzen is much more significant than the usual local news bulletin, and is surprising time and again for its wider cultural interest.

5. I find his conclusion easier to accept: "A large part of the reform spirit originated, in Drenthe as in other places, in the desire for the wealth of the Church." Along with Dr. Naarding, the Reverend J. Wattel believes that Drenthe was already Reformed, for the most part, when Willem Lodewijk brought in the Reformation by force, "although the people remained true to the old forms. The people of Drenthe won't desert them readily." See Wattel's articles "De Hervorming in Drenthe" in *Gereformeerde Kerkbode voor Hoogeveen e.o*, June 28 and July 5, 1947.

6. Reitsma and van Veen, *Drenthe*. This meeting was alternately called: "classis," "classis generalis," and (later) "synod," and it made itself more and more independent of the authority of Groningen. The efforts of Groningen and the Stadhouder to unite Drenthe as Classis with part of Groningen were strongly resisted by the Regional Parliament of Drenthe. After many years of strife—until 1619!—Drenthe obtained independence and its own synod.

7. [Note on dialect]

8. Only Coevorden was also alone, but this was probably a different affair.

9. Once a monk named Master Jan van Aken piously covered the ceiling of the church in Sleen with well-executed paintings. This *"broder"* Jan van Aken

did the same in the church of Sellingen. (See G. J. Hoogewerff, *Noord-Nederlandsche Schilderkunst*, Vol. I; 'sGravenhage, 1936.)

10. *Het Ontstaan van de Gemeenten in Drenthe* (Doctoral dissertation, Leiden, November 30, 1934; Haarlem: H. D. Tjeenk Willink & Zoon); see pp. 9ff.

11. For this practice see Professor Edelman, *Harm Tiesing*, p. 363.

12. Quoted by van der Kley, *Volkskarakter*, p. 51.

V

Drenthe's Share in Van Raalte's Colony

A DUTCH "COLONIE-SANS-DRAPEAU"

"The Rev. Van Raalte from Ommen, with a group of emigrants, have embarked from Rotterdam in order to propagate our people and the true faith in the New World." (Kamper Courant of Oct. 5, 1846)

"As for me, I am satisfied with my condition. There are many pious people here. Religion is quite to our liking. On Sundays we attend Rev. Van Raalte's church." (Letter of Hendrik Lanning of Sleen, written in Holland, Michigan, October 12, 1847)

"The Lord has given us room and we have increased in this country." (Letter received from Miss Reka Kamps of Zeeland, Michigan)

A Dutchman who for the first time examines a detailed map of the Dutch colonies in Michigan will undoubtedly rub his eyes in disbelief. For a moment he must think that a roguish, drunk map maker has cut the familiar map of the Netherlands into a jigsaw puzzle. The large body of water is still to the west, and Holland is the center of the country, although it is only a city here. By going five miles eastward one comes to Zeeland, which in turn is situated five and a half miles north of Overisel. And four miles further east there is Vriesland, and two miles to the south, Drenthe. . . , then Groningen, Borculo. . . . The map is truly an indication that the colonists felt patriotism in spite of themselves. These colonists from all the Protestant border provinces felt (to use Picardt's words) that they had been "spewed out."

It is of special interest to this study to examine how the colonists from the province of Drenthe reacted to the American surroundings,[1] which were totally new to them. We wish to see what share they had in the building of van Raalte's colony, which typical characteristics were evident in their new community, and how their Americanization developed.

They arrived in or about 1847. They came in different groups, after a long, dangerous passage, to the freedom of the immense story-book America of Tom Sawyer and Huckleberry Finn,[2] which they helped to build into what it is today. Michigan had not changed its status from a territory to a state until 1837, and the territory of the United States stretched from coast to coast. During the presidency of James Polk (1845-1849) more than three million square kilometers were added! When the largest group of Drenthian emigrants embarked in March 1847, California had just been annexed by the United States; and when Hendrik Lanning of Sleen wrote his first letter from Michigan to the family at home, the American troops had just captured the Mexican capital. Christian America, to which these colonists came, still had to come to terms with many of its problems. There was the problem of Negro slavery in the south, and that of the polygamy of the Mormons, who in 1848 were to build the New Jerusalem on the Salt Flats of Utah. As yet there was no singing in unison of "Onward, Christian Soldiers" from the ranks of the "New Canaan."

For the time being, however, the recently arrived Americans must have restricted their attention to the immediate duties of their own colonies. In his book *Om Vrijheid en Brood (For Freedom and Bread)*,[3] P. J. Risseeuw pictures very clearly how many troubles and difficulties were involved. The romanticized historical information in the book is based mostly on the extensive research of Dr. van Hinte, of which I myself have frequently made use.

It is strange and regrettable that such a preeminent expert as Dr. van Hinte, who traced and recorded with so much devotion all of the Dutch American colonization, was not invited to join the Dutch delegation to the centennial of Holland, Michigan. If the authorities in The Hague had consulted this expert regarding the preparations for the celebration, we would have been spared a press release such as that at the beginning of August: "As is well known, the founders of the city of Holland originated from the said five provinces," that is, Friesland, Overijssel, Gelderland, Utrecht, and Zeeland. It is inexcusable that in this press release the province of Drenthe was not mentioned. It was well known (or one could verify in van Hinte) that the people of Drenthe participated fully in the van Raalte colonization.

The omission was all the more painful to me because, while doing research for this study, I used a newly published book by Professor Albert Hyma, *Albertus C. van Raalte and his Dutch Settlements in the United States.*[4] Here I found material which I combined with the data about the Drenthe emigrants from the confidential reports to the Governor of the Province, and thus made a very surprising discovery concerning the emigrants from Drenthe.[5] "The Vanguard," a group of seven pioneers who arrived on February 9, 1847, were the first to go to the spot chosen for the colony by the Reverend van Raalte to build the town of Holland. Hyma considers these "the group that made history worth noting," and van Hinte calls them "a small group of heroes." The Vanguard consisted of: the Reverend van Raalte, E. Zagers (from Emmen), W. Notting (from Coevorden), J. Lankheet (from Hellendoorn-Nijverdal),[6] J. Laarman (from Coevorden), E. Fredriks (Vreriks, from Emmen) and the wife of W. Notting (from Coevorden). Of these six persons who accompanied van Raalte and built and inhabited the first blockhouse that would one day become the city of Holland, five came from Drenthe.

Van Raalte himself did not live there in the beginning. Until his own house was erected, he found shelter with the Reverend Smith. Smith was a missionary to the Ottawa Indians who were then living in that region in a settlement about two and a half miles from what would become Holland. The same is true of B. Grootenhuis and his wife, other colaborers of van Raalte, who had departed several days before the Seven Pioneers "to blaze the way and make roads from the house of Rev. Smith to the future town of Holland." (I was not able to determine from where this Grootenhuis came.)

The "Seven Pioneers" (van Raalte included) had left their families in Allegan. "Only one woman, Mrs. Notting, accompanied the first group of settlers." She was one of these seven. *Thus, the first wife in the first house in Holland, Michigan, was a Drenthian!* It

The Reverend Smith, the first minister in Drenthe, Michigan.

is a tragedy that she died within a short time, so that the first grave in the colony also had to be that of an immigrant from Drenthe.

The new settlement resembled closely the idyllic nature of the first Christian communities: "When we had the first log house finished, we had our wives brought from Allegan and five families lived in it together, namely, Zagers, Notting, Lankheet, Laarman, and Fredriks. We lived mutually in peace and had all things in common together. What had been bought and brought from Allegan or given us by American friends was put into the common dish . . ." (from the diary of Egbert Fredriks from Emmen in Drenthe, whose comments Professor Hyma calls "highly illuminating"). "Another story of great value to us," Hyma writes, "is penned by Evert Zagers" who also came from Emmen. Both of these writings certainly deserve to be preserved in the old country, through copying or photocopying, out of respect for what the emigrants from Drenthe helped to create there.

In the old country there must undoubtedly be all sorts of interesting documents and data about these pioneers from Drenthe, especially concerning their first acquaintance with the Reverend van Raalte. The early emigrants from the southeastern part of Drenthe must have had contact with van Raalte when he lived in neighboring Ommen (1837-1844), where he was pastor of the Christian Secessionists. Traditionally there were many contacts between these two places, and van Raalte's special liking for Ommen is unmistakable. Even in 1836, when he had just joined the Secessionists, he officiated in Ommen; in 1866, revisiting the Netherlands, he "preached many sermons, especially at Ommen."[7] The followers he obtained from the area of Ommen determined

This picture, taken in 1878, shows ten of the pioneers who settled Holland in 1847. Shown are, from top left to right: 1—Evert Zagers (from Emmen); 2—Hendrik Jan Plaggermans; 3—Teunis Keppel; 4—Hein Vander Haar; 5—Egbert Frederick; 6—Mrs. H. J. Laarman, who later was Mrs. A. Baker; 7—Francis Smith; 8—Manus Lankheet; 9—Mrs. B. Grootenhuis; 10—B. Grootenhuis.

to a great extent the group of his earliest and most faithful companions for the Trek to America, at the time an unknown destination.

We receive further information about Drenthian involvement from the travel account of Jan Hendrik Stegink, merchant from Borger in Drenthe (preserved by Versteeg in his *Pilgrim Fathers from the West*). It appears that when the rumor spread that the Reverend van Raalte was making preparations to sail for America (1846) with emigrants from the provinces of Overijssel and Gelderland, Evert Zagers and Egbert Fredriks from Emmen traveled to van Raalte. They went to obtain further information, and then decided, along with some other families in and around Coevorden, to undertake the journey with van Raalte.

The following account is a summary of the part played by Drenthians in building up the new colony.

The town of Holland was founded first; in addition to van Raalte, four settlers financed the purchase of the land for the establishment of the city, each of them buying eighty acres. One of them, Jan Rabbers, was a carpenter from Emmen who left there in 1846. (He was not considered well-to-do in Emmen. I wonder if he might possibly be the man about whom the *Drentsche Courant* [October 16, 1846] reported that a departing emigrant from Noordbarge was given 10,000 guilders to buy land in North America by a farmer from Groningen who could not arrange his affairs in time. I do not know if Rabbers came from Noordbarge, a village in the municipality of Emmen; however, his traveling companion, Willem Kremers, did, as I was told by Kremer's son.)

After the foundation of Holland, the villages of Zeeland, Vriesland, Drenthe, Groningen, and Graafschap were established. The founding of Zeeland was financed primarily by J. van de Luyster, a very rich farmer from the province of Zeeland. Some people from Drenthe also settled there.

Drenthe was founded by a number of settlers from Drenthe and some from Staphorst. "There were men of means among these settlers, especially Lanning (Hendrik Lanning, farmer from Sleen) and Broekman (from ?). They had considerable capital and can be recognized as fathers of this settlement. They were those who furnished loans, and who enabled those of lesser means to clear their land."[8] "They were also the relief of Vriesland. Whenever those people were in need, they went to Drenthe, worked in the woods, made fences, and could in this way earn their living and clear their land" (Versteeg).

"Four miles east of Holland the industrious village of Groningen came into being, founded by a Drenthian, the enterprising Jan Rabbers, and later populated by a number of people from the province of Groningen."[9]

And, finally, the village of Graafschap was founded by people from Graafschap-Bentheim in Germany. In the chapter "The Followers of the Rev. De Cock in Drenthe," we saw how closely the Reformed Secessionists were related to Bentheim. In these new villages there were also settlers from the provinces of Drenthe, Gelderland, and Zeeland.[10]

Although they were living in the midst of very dense forests, the lumber they needed had to be floated in from elsewhere, because they lacked a sawmill. Again it was Jan Rabbers from Drenthe who, during the winter of 1847-1848, took the initiative to build one in his village of Groningen. His mill was used by the various communities but had much bad luck; the strong current destroyed the dam several times, and they finally had to give up using the mill. "Rabbers, who was always cheerful and good-natured and a pillar of the colony, afterwards started a flour mill, while one of his neighbors, J. Kolvoort, built a similar mill in the new village of Groningen a little to the north."[11] Rabbers was also the first to open a store in Groningen. Likewise, H. Stokking, who in March 1847 had closed his smithy and farm at Erm, Drenthe, was the first blacksmith in the colony (according to a letter written to me by Nick Hunderman, son of the emigrant G. J. Hunderman from Erm). One can well imagine how important such establishments were in a new colony far away from the civilized world.

Finally, we must make special mention of the significance for van Raalte's venture of the arrival of "men of means," such as the three well-to-do farmers from Sleen who arrived in 1847: Lanning, Riddering, and Weggemans. We know from the confidential reports to the Governor that between the three of them they brought a sum of about 31,000 guilders. What this meant to van Raalte at that time can be readily understood when reading Professor Hyma's chapter "Financing the Pioneer Colony."[12] Van Raalte himself made grateful mention of the fact in his lecture of 1872 (on the occasion of the silver jubilee of the colony): "God's hand was apparent in

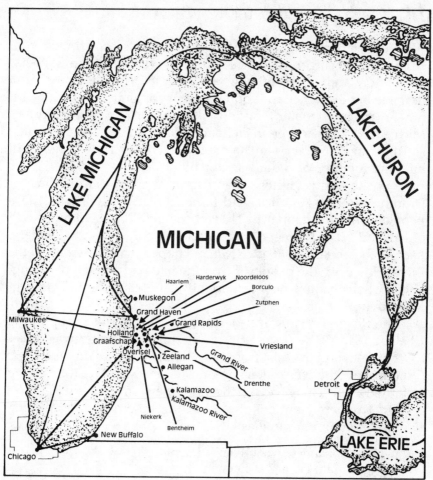

The Van Raalte Trek

the material things of life. Whenever food became scarce, new
sources of supply were provided, and when funds became ex-
hausted, new immigrants arrived with the necessary cash."[13]

Although the settlers from Drenthe contributed their share to
the entire colony, most of them settled in the town of Drenthe.
What were their reactions to their new circumstances? Jan Hendriks
Stegink, a merchant from Borger, tells us about their journey via
Albany, where they spent most of the winter of 1846-1847 (in
Versteeg's *Pilgrim Fathers*).[14] From the Rotary Club of Holland
(Michigan) I received the "Memories of the Beginning of Drenthe,
Michigan," written in 1913 by Henry Kremers, M.D., son of Willem
Kremers who, as a 28-year-old farmhand, set out from Emmen
(Noordbarge) for New York in 1846.

From Dr. Kremers' *Memories* it is clear that the emigration from Drenthe to Michigan found its source in Ommen: "Jan Rabbers, my father, and a few others had become acquainted with the dominie in the Netherlands and were very anxious to go, and with nine men (no women) undertook the trip [from Albany] to Michigan." They arrived in Holland in March 1847, and there they sat once again under van Raalte's preaching. They assisted in building a house of cedar logs for him.

"In the spring of 1848 many farmers from the province of Drenthe came to America, and father joined himself with these people of his acquaintance. They chose good land, 10 miles east of Holland" (Dr. Kremers). "Their fellow countryman, J. Rabbers, had purchased land on Black River and hoped that they would settle there. However, the people of Drenthe had had enough of sailing, and wished in their new fatherland to till clay soil" (Versteeg-Moundyke).

The Reverend A. Keizer dates the arrival of this group in the "Fall of 1847." The first settler at the place that later was called "Drenthe" was Jan Hulst from Staphorst, Overijssel in June 1847. Others arrived a week later, among whom was Arend Smeding (a farmer from Hoogeveen), the first one from Drenthe.

Dr. Kremers mentions the following nine names of the first Drenthian emigrant families:

> Opholt, Johannes; wool dyer at Emmen, 48
> Wiggers, Jan; laborer at Emmen, 35
> Nijenhuis, Jacob; farmer at Westerbork, 58
> Ensink, maid at Sleen, 25 (and family?)
> Lanning, Hendrik; farmer at Sleen, 56
> Riddering, Jan; farmer at Sleen, 59
> Lubbers, Hendrik; laborer at Emmen, 44; with his brother Geert, also
> laborer at Emmen, 38
> Hunderman, Hendrik; farmer at Coevorden, 67; with his son (?)
> Klaas, farmhand at Sleen, 32
> Kamps, Jan; carpenter at Zweelo, 26

To these nine must be added:

> Kremers himself, Willem; farmhand at Emmen, 28
> Brinks, Roelof; farmhand at Emmen, 27 (addition from "Recollections
> of Riek Bouws: Life History of Roelof Brinks")[15]
> Smeding, Arend; farmer at Hoogeveen, 50 (according to the
> Reverend A. Keizer, *The Settlement of Drenthe*)

and further Jan Hulst of Staphorst, who was, of course, actually number one. All were accompanied by their families.[16]

The first controversy that arose was between the Drenthians who lived in the eastern part of the town of Drenthe and the people of Staphorst, who settled in the western part. "Mr. Hulst was the leader of this party and had nailed a board to a tree on his farm with the writing 'Here begins Staphorst.' The old grandfather Hunderman fought hard for Drenthe, and they finally chose that name" (Dr. Kremers). They apparently agreed with the Reformed Synod of the Old Territory of Drenthe of 1598 (the first after the Reformation), which listed under the names of the villages in Drenthe also Staphorst and Roveen, as spiritually belonging to Drenthe.

This contrariness, so typical among neighboring villages in Drenthe, would be aggravated in church affairs. Henry Kremers continues:

> At the east and west the people were organized into one Reformed Church which was served by the pastors of the nearby churches. But they much desired to have their own pastor. One of the party of the west part (Staphorst) was acquainted with a Rev. Roelof Smit from Rumveen [i.e. Rouveen, near Staphorst]. A call was extended to him and he accepted the call (1851). The dominie was a good and well meaning man, but had not had the opportunity to attend school for any length of time and favored the people settled in the eastern part with the result *that they attended church in greater numbers, and this, as is peculiar of the Hollanders, caused great bitterness among the two parties* so that the church was divided. Those of the party living in the western part joined themselves with the United Presbyterian Church and hereafter were called the "Schotsche Kerk."

Three comments before we let Dr. Kremers continue his account:

1. "As is peculiar of the Hollanders"—the Drenthians? "It's a shame that so few of our people go to church," a housewife says to the farmhand in the Drenthe short story *Folmers and His Contemporaries.*

2. As the Reverend Henry Beets, D.D., the well-known church historian, wrote me: "Rev. Roelof Smit desired to become a preacher and obtained some training for this under *Walter Kok* and his assistant." This means that Smit studied theology in Ruinerwold or in Hoogeveen, and thus was influenced by the more rigid

"northern" way of thinking, whereas those from Drenthe were more "southern minded," as we saw before. This contrast seems to continue in the New World. But were those of Staphorst not all followers of the same van Raalte? It seems, therefore, that it must have been more a matter of clannishness!

3. As to the opposing factions in Drenthe, Dr. Beets informed me further: "When the classis met in 1853, there was a complaint against him (Smit), namely, of *promoting factions.*" Now Dr. Kremers continues: "Those living in the eastward part [the Drenthians] remained with the Reformed Church and had no pastor until 1861. Then candidate Roelof Pieters accepted their call. Rev. Smit remained pastor of the '*Schotsche Kerk*' until his death. Many of his parishioners left him and joined the Secession Church at Vriesland. Later, during the secession of 1882, the Reformed Church joined the Secession Church and the Vriesland Church broke up and with those living in Drenthe were anew joined in what is now a strong, flourishing congregation of the Christian Reformed Church."

The Drenthians thus remained longest in the "Dominie van Raalte Church," but *as a group* they accepted, without objection, transfer into a larger church affiliation, although there had been opposition to the *first* association with an *American* religious community (van Hinte, p. 395).

Kremer concludes as follows:

> The separation of the peoples living in the western part and the eastern part assumed such proportions that they had little in common. They each had their own school (Dutch) and besides that, each had their own cemetery. I still remember that one of the Secessionists was asked to have a cemetery lot with the Reformed Church because they had the best cemetery. He was angry and returned the answer, "You do not wish to be with us alive, and we refuse to have you when you are dead." This was the answer of but one individual. However, there was so much opposition that it did not prevail. The public school could not be divided, and here one must come in contact with the other. This helped to establish a better understanding and after 60 years all this is forgotten and the people are united.

How we would like to have more data on the differing conduct of the various groups in the various settlements! Here we are dealing with a sizable sociological project: From all the Protestant border provinces of the Netherlands small groups of religiously like-minded Secessionists are transplanted to a colony with enormous initial difficulties. Do they all react in the same way to the experiment, or do the people from Drenthe, Groningen, Overijssel, Gelderland, Zeeland, and Bentheim react quite differently? [. . .]

I found one striking thought in the Reverend A. Keizer's book: "As far as division among the early settlers is concerned, history mentions two, the secession of 1857 and of 1882. These divisions were the result, except in Drenthe, not of clannishness but of religious viewpoints."

"Except in Drenthe." That means that it was clannishness there, just as in the old country, where the idea of village community dominates to the point of hostility toward other villages. "Whereas in their own village a strong disposition for cooperation prevails, the negative—almost hostile—attitude toward other villages is all the more striking" (van der Kley). Notwithstanding "1847," the people from Drenthe remained Drenthians. With all their internal quarrels, they remained a village community united against the other villages. And the means that the Drenthians used in their new country appear to be no less drastic than in the old Drenthe. Thus van hinte relates: "When the Rev. R. Smit preached for his Staphorst people on religious holidays, the Drenthian brethren decided to cut down trees so close to the church that they disturbed the services."

In spite of all the quarreling, the settlements grew. When the Reverend I. N. Wyckoff visited the different villages in 1849, Holland with its surroundings had 235 houses, Zeeland 175, Groningen 30, Drenthe 45, Vriesland 69, Overisel 35, and Graafschap 20—a total of 639 homes, with about 3,000 inhabitants (van Hinte, p. 240). Moreover, about 3,000 acres of forest had been cut down, and these were being readied for occupation.

This expansion had many aspects that might lead to different reactions. The first communal work (the building of van Raalte's house, the hacking out of roads, the building of a bridge across the Black River) was done without payment (van Hinte, pp. 242-243). Did this suit the Drenthians better than the other settlers, accustomed as they were to farm work? For the Grand Haven bridge, however, there was need of some gentle pressure. Those who stayed away had to pay $1.50 a day as compensation or hire a competent worker as a substitute. The earliest transportation and commercial enterprises in the colony were conducted on a cooperative base (including provisions, household articles, and tools). However, these cooperatives failed, since they were no match for the development of private enterprise, as favored by, for example, Jan Rabbers. If we only knew more about the various reactions!

How important the church controversy in Drenthe must have been can be judged from the fact that the consistory in the villages (not in Holland) controlled all government, including secular affairs. As John Shoemaker of Zeeland, Michigan (grandson of Klaas Shoemaker of Sleen) informed me: "The church was the government of the community. All the people belonged to the church and so she would decide many of the local matters. Later on, as the inhabitants increased, the people were not all members of the church. Then, too, they became more Americanized and took to the federal courts for their settlements of troubles."

This submission to accepted authority was more characteristic of the Drenthians and the related Saxon people than of the people of Zeeland. When the colony newspaper *De Hollander* voiced opposition to the "theocratic" tendencies of van Raalte and his consistory, the Drenthians stood behind van Raalte when Doesburg (the publisher) was denied admittance to the Lord's Supper. The Zeelanders remained neutral.

As for possible political interests on the part of his grandfather's descendants, John Shoemaker wrote me: "As far as I know, none have held any political office unless it was some minor township office. Most of them were not too deeply interested in politics." This lack of interest is apparent from the "wholesale naturalization" of the Drenthians to permit participation in the election of 1851. As for the other communities, there were three hundred applicants in Holland, one hundred in Zeeland, and forty in Vriesland.

Those first elections, held in Zeeland, led to unfortunate bickering. All sorts of grievances and differences were aired on that occasion. First, there was protest against the supremacy of van Raalte and his theocracy, and then there was the contrast between the "city" people and the villagers. The villagers usually spoke rather acrimoniously of "the city" of Holland. Van Hinte quotes: "The men of Zeeland and Stateland (that is, the village of Drenthe and surroundings) were full of anger at the city men of Holland" (Vol.

I, p. 257). Were the Drenthians, the so-called "Statelandmen," involved after all?

Meanwhile, the American Drenthe developed, from an economic point of view, into a true Drenthian agrarian village. Mr. Leon N. Moody, secretary of the Holland Rotary Club in Holland, Michigan, wrote to me: "It is now only a small community. I go there on occasion to buy cream and butter for my family use." And Mr. Nick Hunderman (the son of the Drenthe emigrant G. J. Hunderman) describes his hometown thus: "A small village, one church, school, garage, store, creamery, and shoemaker. *Mostly all farmers.*" I also asked Mr. S. Koning of Assen, who was to visit his brother in Grand Rapids, to make a trip to Drenthe to take a series of snapshots. He told me that the differences between the provinces of origin are still noticeable. The Drenthians, more than the others, cling to community and family. And the Drenthian still prefers the horse to the tractor. And Mrs. Nick Lanning of Grand Rapids says: "The people in Drenthe are still rather frugal, but of course the younger generation has a different life-style from the older. Most of them have new houses, fine furniture, and everyone has a car, and it takes quite a bit to do all of that. I think most of the Drenthians are curious people and don't have much to say. But on the whole they are good people."

Although Drenthe kept its agrarian character, it is interesting to determine to what extent the descendants of the settlers continued farming. Mr. John Shoemaker wrote me as follows: "My grandfather and his children were all farmers, of the grandchildren there were 8 that had farms (all retired now except 2), of the more than 65 great-grandchildren there are only four that till the soil."

I was especially intrigued by a detailed survey of the descendants of Hendrik Lanning from Sleen, which was sent to me by his great-grandson, Nick Lanning, from Grand Rapids. The survey of occupations, however, is rather incomplete. It nevertheless appears that various farmers named Lanning still live in Drenthe, such as Nicklas, Albert, and Kenneth.

It is interesting to trace the Americanization of the descendants of this patriarch Hendrik Lanning. The survey reports: 2 children, 14 grandchildren, 36 great-grandchildren, about 60 great-great-grandchildren, and even a number of great-great-great-grand-children. From the marriage records it appears that until the fourth generation, that is, until about 1940, these descendants married almost exclusively people of Dutch descent; practically all the family names of spouses are Dutch. The Christian names show a stronger Americanization. The second generation was still one hundred percent Dutch, the third about half, with Geesje next to Mabel, Hendrik next to Clifford. But the fourth generation shows no Drenthian names anymore: Harold, Harry, Evelyn, Gerald, Elizabeth, Harriet, Norajane, Shirley Ann, Ruthie, Nicklas Jr., Alger, Henry George, Lu Ann, and Harvey. The same is found in the fifth generation. "They are no longer named after grandmother or grandfather; sometimes only the first letter remains, but never the full name." This pattern proves that English has become the language of the descendants. My correspondents, however, are an exception to this rule: "Of the whole family, I am the only one who still writes a little Dutch. [The "little" is not true; the Dutch is quite correct.] Most people are still able to talk Dutch, even most of our children, which makes me feel rather proud. For none of the children of Nick's brothers and sisters can. But Nick and I always kept it up. At home we talk Dutch. . . ."

Finally, it is noteworthy that the spread of descendants across the United States has remained rather limited. And as to church affiliation, they nearly all belong either to the Reformed or the Christian Reformed Church.

NOTES

1. Where it was possible "to imagine oneself in Drenthe" (Van Hinte, I, 210).

2. Just as Mark Twain pictured this for the southern areas of the U.S.A.

3. Published by Bosch en Keuning, Baarn, 1947.

4. Dr. Albert Hyma, born in the Netherlands, is Professor of History at The University of Michigan. The book was published by Wm. B. Eerdmans Publishing Co., Grand Rapids, 1947.

5. See "Drente," August 1947.

6. The suspicion that here we had someone from Overijssel was correct, according to research in the Archives at Zwolle. Dr. B. H. Slicher van Bath found various Lankheets as emigrants. Hermannus Lankheet emigrated before 1847. I therefore put a question mark by the initial of his first name. See also Dr. J. van Hinte, *Nederlanders in Amerika*, Vol. I. He already mentioned this "vanguard" (without place of origin): "We may speak of a small band of heroes, if we recall this apparently unimpressive little group of six men and one woman . . . ," and among them J. Lankheet.

7. See Professor Hyma, *Van Raalte*, p. 225.

8. D. Versteeg, *The Pilgrim Fathers of the West* (Grand Rapids, 1886).

9. Van Hinte, I, p. 158. Character sketch of Jan Rabbers in Versteeg, *The Pilgrim Fathers*, pp. 159ff.

10. *Van Hinte*, I, p. 158.

11. *Van Hinte*, I, p. 248.

12. *Hyma*, pp. 146ff., especially p. 163.

13. Hyma, p. 251. See also the anecdote concerning Jan Rabbers (Versteeg, p. 161) and the usual question he asked new arrivals, "Did you bring along any money?"

14. See Van Hinte, I, pp. 64 and 244.

15. Supplied by the secretary of the Holland Rotary Club.

16. To get an idea of life in the village of Drenthe in the early days, it is interesting to read a letter dated November 10, 1849, from H. Scheepers, who emigrated with his family to North America, to those left behind in Hijken. The letter was printed in the *Drentsche Courant* of April 5, ff., 1850. "This man was known for his great dependability in his former hometown," commented the editor in his introduction. In this letter we meet the following emigrants from Drenthe: Koos Eleveld, five Vredevelds, Berent Kamps, Jan van Ree, Van Dammen (both from Zuidlaren), Roelof Weurdinge, Gerrit van Ree, Harm Kruit, the Ten Haves, Hendrik Pijl, Klaas Boer, Wolter Schoenmaker, Albert Weurding, Hinderman (from Coevorden), the smith Stokkens; from Emmen, Opholt, Jan Wiggers, Willem Kremer, Albert Lubberts, Geert Lubberts, Lanning from Erm, Jan and Hendrik Kamps, Jan Heuving, Jacob and Roelof Neyenhuis. This Scheepers from Hijken played an important role in the new community. "We live a half-hour south of the church; we have no preacher yet; I am instructing several people in the truth of godliness and the hope of eternal life."

17. See comment 2 in the text.

VI

Schism in the Village Communities of Drenthe

"The freedom of country life is an illusion of the city dweller. It is real to him only as long as he doesn't belong to the village community. That community demands strict adherence to its laws and customs."

(P. W. J. van den Berg)

The Coercive Nature of Drenthian Village Communities

The quotation above from the well-known folklore scholar Dr. P.W.J. van den Berg is no doubt based on personal experience in the province of Drenthe, to which he devoted all of his life as a pastor, serving the Reformed Church in a variety of functions. The book from which this quotation is taken is said to be especially inspired by Drenthe.[1]

On what does this compelling character of the communities of Drenthe rest? Harm Tiesung assures us that the faithfully observed neighbor duties were never regulated by law. However, I recently happened to come across such a regulation from the Stellingwerfse area: a written "Regulation containing rules of duties in the case of death in the neighborhood of Boekhorst and Kampen," with fines for neglect of the keeping of the neighbor duties. Included were annotations regarding the keeping of the regulations from 1897 to 1922. J. Poortman mentions a similar instance in Zuidwolde. Does anyone know about more of these in Drenthe? Dr. Naarding knows about them in Groningen. For the sake of history this issue requires separate research. For this study we will restrict ourselves to Dr. van den Berg.

In Drenthe the power of public opinion is based on the idea that "what has always been done here by everyone is how it ought to be done," as van den Berg describes the norm of behavior in the village.[3] And the consequence of refusing to conform was (and still is) complete ostracism. Such a person "is forced to move; no tradesman dares to deliver anything at his house; if need be, his house is demolished right over his head."[4] Didn't it occur recently that for Liberation Day celebrations the decorations along the road were omitted very noticeably at the house of someone who had not observed local customs? The youth of a village may take justice into their own hands even today (cf. the story in *Hilde* by the Drenthian novelist, Anne De Vries).

In the days of the Secession the same means were used in Drenthe. Frederik Kok, later the pastor of the Christelijke Gereformeerden, was at the time still a shopkeeper in Dwingelo. When he no longer attended the village church, but organized services in his house, the village community began to agitate against him. "Time and again they (that is, fellow villagers) smashed our windows. In the evening or at night they riddled them with bullets, so that we finally put in no more new windows, but boarded them up with planks or paper. When this happened at night, we didn't even get out of bed any more, and when in the evening, we no longer went out of doors. We hardly dared to do so anyway, because it sometimes happened that a shower of stones came as soon as we came out. . . . Frederik's business was almost ruined. Once, when we were away, some men broke into his house, rifled his whole shop, and buried everything in a woods outside of Dwingeloo."[5]

There is a remarkable contrast in the case of Master Albert (mentioned above) when he also walked out of the church in Dwingeloo some years later:

> On the following Sunday Master Albert was again in church in Dwingeloo. He had read the Scripture and the pastor began his sermon. He preached again, as I was told, missing the truth. And . . . suddenly Master Albert rose, put on his hat and calmly left the church. What a consternation! They understood what he meant. And as if many had been waiting for it, most of the congrega-

tion got up and followed him out of the church. As a thunderclap the cry rang out through the village: Oh! oh! what will come of it! Master Albert walked out of church and the whole congregation followed him!

Evidently Master Albert's authority within the congregation was considerably greater than that of the minister—who played the role of the "strange duck in the pond." In both the Kok and the Master Albert instances the antagonism was directed against the one who was suddenly branded as the violator of the prevailing standards of the community.

The account of the people's justice on the stubborn Frederik Kok came from the Secessionist camp. But there is also an account from the other camp, as contained in the "Letter of Van Bobbel," former corporal of the "Riflemen of Sasse," to the Bailiff from Drenthe [Uncle Berend, a famous character from the Podagrist literature], during the latter's stay in Amsterdam. The account takes place in 1843, is fictional, but obviously is based on real life, and is written in the style of Dickens' *Pickwick Papers*.

Just imagine that the other day some sort of evangelist from G. visited our village, one of those De Cock characters, you know. You could tell that he was a little crazy, the way he squinted out of his eyes. Well, that fellow wanted to conduct a service or something here in our village to save souls from the clutches of the Evil One, as he said, because right and pure doctrine was not preached here and our pastor was a modernist who seduced the sheep. I thought to myself, what's all this about modernist and clutches of the Evil One and pure doctrine. I couldn't stand it that our honest, good dominie was belittled and slandered by such a queer duck! And when in the evening that pious fellow was ready to start his godly work (as he thinks of it) at Lambert Snider's (who, as you know, also belongs to the pious) do you know what I did, Uncle Berend? I unexpectedly entered the room where they intended to perform the farce. I had my manpower with me, a crew of about forty or fifty husky farmhands—your Arend being one of them. I had arranged beforehand that they should pick up the master hairsplitter bodily and carry him outside the village. Well, it went off without a hitch! Before the fool realized what was going on, he was sitting on a thresher outside the barn door, whether he wanted to or not. We took him in a long procession, all the while singing, past the parsonage, out of the village, into the fields, where we let the lout go, telling him that he better never return or he'd get even worse treatment. When coming by the parsonage they had tossed him up and down, shouting, "Long live our dominie!" and "Away with the head-droopers!" We made him join in, which he did. My goodness, Uncle Berend, this whole affair was just grist for my mill. My old corporal's heart starts to beat again as if it were thirty years younger. I am sure that you, too, being fond of the dominie, will enjoy hearing that the young fellows at my suggestion to a man took the side of their pastor and threw that foreign skunk out in a way he won't dare mention to anyone, for if he does, there isn't a bit of shame in him.

Uncle Berend, the Assessor, comments on this story of his friend Corporal van Bobbel: "This should happen to all those foreign birds that come to disturb the peace and unity in the community with their self-righteous preaching," thereby giving his official sanction to the "peace and justice" the youths in his Hondsrug village had achieved by their village justice against the Secessionists.

The social disciplinary effect of such village justice (as the people of Dwingeloo administered to Frederik Kok, and Corporal van Bobbel to the guest of Lambert Snider) is beyond dispute. Is it any wonder that a novelty, such as the first artificial fertilizer, was spread on the fields by night, from fear that the neighbors might take offence at it?[6]

Even in our days it still happens in those Drenthian villages that have remained rather isolated, that every infringement on the unity of the lifestyle is strongly resented. This was all the more so in earlier times when the very isolated village life was far more static. Many a case of individual emigration may have been caused by an inability to conform. And those who stayed behind became all the more conservative because of this selectivity and, as a village community, became an ideal example of organic group life.

Yet, as Copernicus said, "nevertheless it moves." In every human society a steady change takes place, the kind of change that can be best studied at the line of fracture of a schism, which in turn means the beginning of a new group formation.

How Is a Schism Comprehensible?

How then is a schism comprehensible in such a strongly bound Drenthian village community? The prominent Dr. Benthem Reddingius of Assen declared in 1840: ''Wherever these faults are present (fanaticism, denunciation of others, and a tendency toward secession), especially in the peat-colonies but also elsewhere, the seeds of it are spread by people who came from outside and did not belong to the Drenthian clans. The people of Drenthe are, on the whole, religious in a reasonable way.''[7] Granted that Drenthe from Dr. Picardt's day until the present more than once proved to be susceptible to and in need of a push from the outside— prophets are usually more successful outside their own country—I must nevertheless emphasize that Master Albert and his sons, and later the Michigan emigrants from southeast Drenthe, certainly belonged to the clans of Drenthe. Dwingeloo and Diever, and certainly the old villages from where the Lannings hailed (Erm, etc.), should definitely not be considered part of the peat colonies. The intellectual Dr. Benthem Reddingius was, of course, especially irritated by the activity of the peat digger ''Dominee Luxien'' of Smilde, and his argument seems to be directed primarily against him. This Luxien Dijkstra was indeed an outsider. He was born about 1799 in Gorredijk, Friesland, and married Grietje Eendvogel from Smilde. Their first child was born about 1825.

No, the church controversies of those days did not pass over the heads of the people of Drenthe. But a recurring question does arise: Who indeed should be considered a true Drenthian? Should our regional author Harm Tiesing, for instance? But his grandfather was born in Bentheim, ''one of those who left their native country because of poverty, to find a good escape in Drenthe, which they did not consider so poor.''[8] It would be interesting to trace the ancestors of the first Drenthian Secessionists and of the emigrants to Michigan in the same way. This might possibly reveal a greater mobility of the population, which might lead to speculations about a certain mobility of the character of the people in the course of the centuries. For the time being, I feel safe in regarding the Koks of Eemster and the Lannings of Erm as true Drenthians, born, grown up, and accepted as full members of their respective village communities. How, then, did these people come to such a schism, so alien to the Drenthian character?

The tension between Calvinism and Humanism has been a feature of Dutch church life ever since the Reformation. Remonstrants and Contra-Remonstrants, Coccejans and Voetians,

Compromisers and Fanatics, Modernists and Conservatives—new names appear for the representatives of the two doctrinal poles. In the course of time these two extremes may become active and then again go into hiding in books, but then suddenly take on a new shape again and inspire new representatives. A religious revival certainly does not always require inspiration from outside; it can grow as a germ from the inside—even in Drenthe—and then discover spiritual kinship elsewhere.

The church annals of Drenthe reveal concern about purity of doctrine already in the first years of the Reformation. In 1613, for instance, at the Classis General of Assen the question arose if there were a need "to prevent and to eliminate all errors or heresies with regard to pure doctrine of the Word of God." And the answer was that "this is very necessary." At that time, however, it was the ministers who were concerned about such questions; there is no mention of the laity raising questions. Nevertheless, the controversy of Calvinism versus Humanism gradually took hold of the church-goers of Drenthe. Master Albert is a classic example. One can see how his concern penetrated the common people in Tillema's book *Folmers and his Contemporaries*, which is a good reconstruction of the social setting in the 1820s. The book deals with the effect of the new school system, improved transportation, and slander—although Master Folmers is too much idealized and Snieder Rieks too much of a caricature.

Although this tension was in principle present during the Reformation, it is remarkable that in the first half of the nineteenth century the Calvinists in Drenthe grew from a loosely connected group without much adhesion to a far more consolidated group, which ignored the borders of parish and village community. Older Christian Reformed people still can tell how their parents from Sleen, for instance, were baptized in Meppen in a room where services were held. Such an act must have violated the social standards of a community such as Erm or Sleen.

Mr. J. T. Linthorst Homan, former Commissioner of the Queen, once remarked that with World War I the door of the "old Drenthe" was closed. Whatever truth is in this remark, it is certainly true that, from the other side, the door had been opened much earlier as an entrance gate to the "new Drenthe"—although hardly noticed by many people at first.

In the "old Drenthe" the village community was the only social order. Actually, one was born into it, just as one is born into the primary life circle, the family (which in Drenthe continued long as a patriarchal relationship). And one also belonged automatically to a well-defined agrarian community, the *boerschap* (farmer society), to the all-inclusive church and school community, and to the general authority of the *eigenerfden* (land-possessing representatives) who directed the civil as well as the ecclesiastic affairs of the neighborhood, cultivation of the common lands, local justice, and defense against common danger such as fire, wolves, and so forth. For one born into the community, life was practically impossible outside of it; once set free he was an outlaw.

Perhaps a single Jewish family admitted to the village formed a certain break in this tight unity. But this was accepted as something of a biblical curiosity, and no one would have thought of assuming such an exceptional position for himself.

It was in the Napoleonic era that this innate sense of unity was shaken—first by the preceding revolutionary disturbances of the *Keezen*, and later by the reconstruction of the state constitution. The separation of religious, civil, and agrarian authority was the most crucial factor. The beginning of the separation of church and state put the *kerkespraak* outside the church walls. This *kerkespraak* had served the people both as newspaper and radio and provided all the necessary information, also concerning civil affairs. In addition, civil weddings were introduced, which largely replaced church weddings. The authority figures among the farmers were no longer by the same token the church authorities, as at the beginning of the Reformation and presumably a long time afterwards. The formation of incorporated municipalities brought new authorities into the local community, and the "assessors," later called councilmen of the municipality, made their appearance beside the *volmachten*.[9]

Traditionally, all authority over the affairs of each village community belonged to certain freeholders; for centuries the same families occupied the same farms and the same positions. Inspired by rationalistic ideas, this authority was now gradually divided along new lines, into various offices held by different persons.

Thus, the traditional authority in the old Drenthian village communities had been shaken severely at the beginning of the nineteenth century. The "progress" of that time, applauded by the so-called Podagrists, also promoted the construction of canals and roads, which furthered the improvement of transportation between towns. Like-minded individuals therefore made contact with each other sooner. The school system, which was much improved during the French era, brought better education; in Drenthe the school improvement was strongly promoted by Bailiff Hofstede (later Governor of the King). But the change also met with opposition, since it was considered government interference with what traditionally had been the business of the *boerschap*.

The rest was accomplished by the measures of King William I, and, closer to home, by the attitudes of superiority among the upper class and the arrogance of the "thinking ones in the nation" (these attitudes were soon adopted by the general public). There might not have been such splintering in Drenthe if the upper classes had not reacted so vehemently in speeches and writings (which were still rather new in the province of Drenthe). This group, which considered itself broad-minded, had no eye for a possible plurality of Christian belief.

The search for spiritual support, begun perhaps at first by a harmless visit to a conventicle, was blown up to be an activity dangerous to the state. In the archives of Smilde one can read how in the 1830s Mayor Kymmell proposed severe persecution to the Governor. ("Cowardly application of a coercive Napoleonic law to harmless meetings"—that is how Kymmell was judged by the opposition's paper, the *Kamper Courant*, which was by no means Calvinistically oriented, since it was the mouthpiece of the rising liberal movement). And many a person who considered himself to be a good member of his village community and who faithfully performed his neighborly duties, must suddenly have felt that he, to his dismay, belonged to two greatly different social communities. Alongside the traditional authority in the village community, albeit weakened by rationalistic divisions, another authority of a charismatic character presented itself: before 1834 Master Kok and his sons, around 1834 the Reverend de Cock and his adherents, and around 1847 the Reverend van Raalte.

To what extent people looked for support in these new groups can still be sensed from letters I was able to read from figures such as Hendrik Lanning and Jantje Buuls. ("She must have been the strong influence in the home," her grandson John Shoemaker wrote to me.)

Of course, these followers did not voluntarily separate themselves from the village community in order to enter a new group.
When faced with opposing communities, it appears that they just
instinctively preferred a charismatic authority over a tradition that
was deteriorating into rationalistic dominance. It is interesting to
note that the preference in both cases tended toward authority of
a religious nature.

The history recounted above may disprove, for this group at
least, the idea that religious faith does not effect the Drenthian emo-
tionally very much. But van der Kley's mention of a "lack of personal character" in church life in Drenthe must be compared with
what I found in the course of my research in the opposite camp.
As I see it, the feeling for organic cohesion of the local community
is as a rule so dominant that the cultural traditions are usually maintained as long as possible, and this also in the area of the church—as
long as it can be done in peace. The Drenthian remains in the one
community as long as he can, even when there are deeply felt
divergent religious convictions.

If some disturbance arises in the community, he will first of
all turn instinctively against the alleged disturber. Thus, the intru-
sion upon the prayer meeting at Dwingeloo was a village rebellion
against the antisocial Freerk, while the marching out of church by
the popular Master Albert became a village action against the
minister, in which even the Squire of Oldengaerde joined. (The
Secessionists then bought him an armchair to replace the family
pew in the village church.) And in Sleen and Erm we saw that the
Reverend Schultz, who by his marriage became more closely tied
to the village community than usual, defended the unity so strongly
and had such strong village support that the dissenters finally left.

In the western part of Drenthe the new parishes of the
Secessionists flourished first; in the old villages of the sandy
southeastern part, the insulting treatment of the Secessionists appears to be a spiritual casting out, which those who would later
become emigrants were no longer able to bear.

In earlier times when village opinion turned against a noncon-
formist, he was finished. During the time of these events transportation had improved, and the printed word brought the news even
to the common man. If he developed a spirit of dissent because
his own value-judgments no longer coincided with the behavior

required by the village community, he was now able to find the support of kindred minds elsewhere. And this tie grew stronger as the pressure increased. The expulsion no longer left the old community unscathed; a new "sectarian" community came into being. The schism had become a reality.

NOTES

1. Dr. P. W. J. van den Berg, *Het Karakter der Plattelandssamenleving,* p. 74.

2. See my article, "De ongeschreven naoberplichten," in *Nieuwe Drentse Volksalmanak,* LXV.

3. *Van den Berg,* p. 75.

4. Van der Kley, *Het Drentse Volkskarakter,* p. 53.

5. *Meister Albert,* p. 56.

6. *Van der Kley,* p. 19.

7. B. Reddingius, *Drentsche Volksalmanak,* 1841. The attribution to the Reverend Reddingius was noted with a question mark by the *Podagrists,* but without it by van der Kley.

8. Edelman, p. 11.

9. See Mr. J. Linthorst Homan, "Het ontstaan van de gemeenten in Drenthe" (Dissertation; Leiden, 1934).

Epilogue

"The wind blows where it wills."
(John 3:8)

Community is a wonderful thing. And schismatic behavior seldom receives sympathy from those who love the community. Nevertheless, every schism gives birth to new forms of community.

The Drenthian is innately a community person, devoted to his own village community and his own soil. By nature he is neither a dissenter nor an emigrant. Yet, during one period of the history of this region we see Drenthians separate into sectarian groups (even though they did so under de Cock's slogan of "return"). Under the constant pressure of the preservers of the unity, a new close unity develops in an accelerated tempo as a result of their common fate. And it is this same pressure that motivates some to participate in the Great Trek to America, where they have an important share in the founding of Holland, Michigan. But once there, they prove to have remained Drenthian in their attachment to the rediscovered village community and to the newly acquired soil.

In a gripping film Professor Steinmetz (the father of Dutch sociography) explained this emigration by the theory of "psychic mutation," while characterizing the emigrants as "weak people" and "poverty stricken, lower-class folk."[1] He was of the opinion that faith could not work this change, and that the attraction of America played a large role. As demonstrated above, Steinmetz started from false premises, at least in our field of study. Moreover, his supposition appears to be inspired by a desire to trace history in main lines and to interpret social events on that basis.

In my opinion we can only record what happened (or, at least, try to do so as well as we can). Then, acknowledging that "the

72

wind blows where it wills," we must try to understand why this emigration took place just at that time—since there are so many aspects that are atypical for Drenthe—and why Drenthe, in the Dutch emigration as a whole, presents such a unique picture.

It must be specifically noted that the fortuitous combination of Drenthian characteristics and Calvinistic principles eminently qualified these Michigan pioneers to become colonists.[2] The sober life-style of the Drenthian combined with the ascetic life-style of de Cock's followers, and the feeling for teamwork in the village community combined with the idea of "sovereignty in one's own sphere." Thus, the firm standards of village life and of Calvinism undoubtedly shaped the disciplined societal forces in the new community. And, finally, respect for authority was only strengthened by these combinations.

The ultimate authority in the community was the Reverend Albertus van Raalte, the man who, according to Professor Hyma, "had a grand vision, such as few mortals ever may attain."[3] The people from Drenthe were more loyal to him than many other settlers, because they had already attached themselves to the new community, even more so than the people from Staphorst, and they repeated the clannish slogan, "Right or wrong, our Drenthe!"

The Drenthian emigrants to Michigan also went "for freedom and bread." In their civic life they especially searched for the commonwealth of the village community that they had lost in their native land. Although they were common people, they must, in their best moments, have understood van Raalte's "It is God's will!" May they have found that *koinonia*, which is presented to us as the highest form of community: "The communion of the Holy Ghost be with you all" (2 Cor. 13:14).

NOTES

1. *Gesammelte Kleinere Schriften zur Ethnologie und Soziologie*, Vol. III, pp. 316–317. "Veranderingen by de Nederlandsche Laudverhuizers in America," based on van Hinte's dissertation.

2. Van Hinte describes the emigrants of the nineteenth century generally as Gerrit Witse types, in contrast to the Jan Huygen characters of the seventeenth century. In relation to the emigrants from Drenthe this comparison appears rather "bourgeois" to me.

3. Hyma, p. 189.

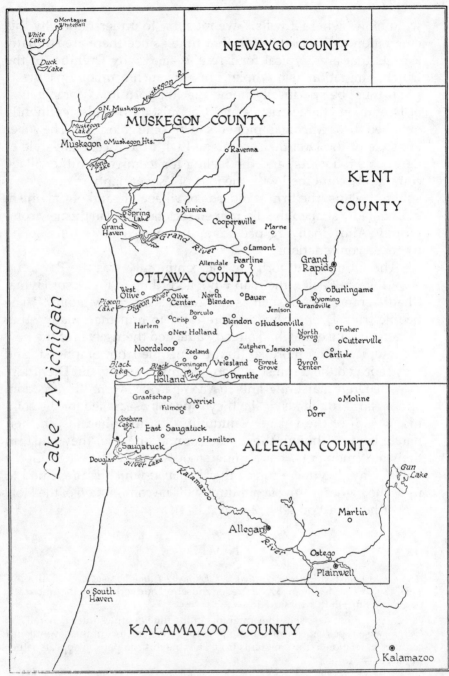

The Michigan Kolonie at its greatest extent (about 1880), showing all the communities except those in Missaukee County, to the northeast. Courtesy of the University of Michigan Press.

Drenthe, Michigan, in the 1980's. Photos by Donald Bruggink.

Appendix I*

A REPORT CONCERNING THE EMIGRANTS
TO NORTH AMERICA

Made at the Provincial Offices at Assen, March 1848

ASSEN:

Dalman, Geert Buning; leather worker; age 41; Secessionist; with wife, 3 children and 1 maid; departed March 9, 1847.

Marlink, Hendrik; carpenter; age 28; Secessionist; unmarried; departed March 9, 1847.

BEILEN:

Koning, Geert; farmer; age 57; Secessionist; with wife and 6 children; departed March 1, 1847.

Ten Have, a widow; farmer; age 59; Secessionist; with 2 children; departed March 16, 1847.

Boer, Klaas; carpenter; age 28; Secessionist; with wife and 1 child; departed March 16, 1847.

Vredeveld, Albert; farmer; age 58; Secessionist; with wife and 6 children; departed March 16, 1847.

Kruid, Jan; tailor; age 68; Secessionist; with 3 children; departed March 16, 1847.

Schuiling, Widdow H.; farmer; age 62; Secessionist; with 1 child; departed March 16, 1847.

Van Nuil, Lucas; laborer; age 26; Secessionist; with wife; departed March 16, 1847.

Bremer, Arend; laborer; age 36; Secessionist; with wife and 1 child; departed March 16, 1847.

BORGER

Stegink, Jan Hendriks; trader; age 34; Secessionist; with wife; departed 1846.

Manting, Geert; baker; age 30; Secessionist; departed 1847.**

Manting, Hendrik; shoemaker; age 21; Secessionist; departed 1847.**

Flories, Lammert; servant; age 27; Secessionist; departed 1847.

*Two of the four Appendixes (*Bijlage* I and II) are reproduced on the following pages. Appendix III consists of a quotation from Versteeg's *Pelgrim-Vaders*. Appendix IV is a poem in the Drenthian dialect, "Van Raalte-Trek, 1847."

**Sons of the local healer Albertus Mantingh of Borger. According to a report from Geert's son Reinardus G. Manting of Holland, Michigan (born 1866), Geert Manting later practiced this same service as his father: "My father settled in Fillmore Township two miles south of Eighth St. (or 40th St.). He was a doctor, the *first doctor in that vicinity.*"

COEVORDEN:
Van Zee, Widow Harm; smith; age 64; Secessionist; with 7 children; departed 1846.
Notting, Willem; dyer; age 35; Secessionist; with wife and 2 children; departed 1846.
Laarman, Widow Jan; farmer; age 64; Secessionist; with 4 children; departed 1846.
Kramer, Louwrens Wispelwey; carpenter; age 43; Secessionist; with wife and 4 children; departed 1847.
Notting, Hendericus; dyer; age 37; Secessionist; with wife and 4 children; departed 1847.
Huyser, Quirinus; farmer; age 30; Secessionist; with wife and 1 child; departed 1847.
Kronemeyer, Berent; carpenter; age 43; Secessionist; with wife and 5 children; departed 1847.
Hunderman, Hendrik; farmer; age 67; Secessionist; with 1 child; departed 1847.
Ter Haar, Berend; farmer; age 21; Secessionist; with wife; departed 1847.

DALEN:
Wessels, Jan Hendrik; farmer; age 33; Roman Catholic; with wife and 4 children; 2 servants; departed 1845.
The Mother-in-law of the above; farmer; Roman Catholic; with 2 children; departed 1845.
Achteren, Berend Hendrik; farmer; age 30; Roman Catholic; with wife and 2 children and 1 servant; departed 1845.
Finder, Johann Wilhelm; farmer; age 42; Roman Catholic; with wife and 7 children; departed 1845.
Taalken, Jan Berends; laborer; age 30; Roman Catholic; with wife and 1 child; departed 1845.
Bruins, Jan Berends; farmer; age 44; Roman Catholic; with wife and 5 children; departed 1845.
The mother-in-law of the above; departed 1845.
Hidding, Hendrik; laborer; age 40; Secessionist; with wife and 3 children; departed 1846.

DWINGELO:
Meyering, Jantien Jans; maid; age 28; Secessionist; departed 1847.

EMMEN:
Rabbers, Jan; carpenter; age 33; Secessionist; with wife and 2 children; departed 1846.
Wassen, Harm; tailor; age 33; Secessionist; with wife and 1 child; departed 1846.
Vreriks, Egbert; laborer; age 36; Secessionist; with wife and 2 children; departed 1846.
Zagers, Evert; laborer; age 36; Secessionist; with wife and 2 children; departed 1846.
Joling, Jan Geerts; tailor; age 47; Reformed; departed 1846.
Brinks, Roelof; farm laborer; age 27; Secessionist; departed 1846.
Kremers, Willem; farm laborer; age 28; Secessionist; departed 1846.
Jekel, Hendrik; farm laborer; age 24; Secessionist; departed 1846.
Lubbers, Hendrik; laborer; age 44; Secessionist; with wife and three children; departed 1847.
Tubbergen, Martinus; carpenter; age 27; Reformed; departed 1847.
Kuypers, Geert; tailor; age 40; Secessionist; with wife and 1 child; departed 1847.

Jekel, Jan Willem; laborer; age 43; Secessionist; with wife and 4 children; departed 1847.

Opholt, Johannes; dyer; age 48; Secessionist; with wife and 3 children; departed 1847.

Wiggers, Jan; laborer; age 35; Secessionist; with wife and 1 child; departed 1847.

Lubbers, Geert; laborer; age 38; Secessionist; with wife and 1 child; departed 1847.

Strabbing, Jan; farm laborer; age 30; Secessionist; departed 1847.

HAVELTE:

Booy, Klaas; carpenter; age 42; Secessionist; with wife and 5 children; departed 1847.

HOOGEVEEN:

Smit, Harm Jans; farmer and peat worker; age 56; Secessionist; with wife; departed 1847.

Smeding, Arend Arends; farmer; age 50; Secessionist; with wife and 4 children; departed 1847.

Sempel, Karst Warners; farmer; age 48; Secessionist; with wife and 6 children; departed 1847.

ODOORN:

Snoek, Jan; laborer; age 35; Secessionist; with wife and 1 child; departed 1846.

Kuypers, Hendericus; laborer; age 35; Secessionist; with wife; departed 1846.

ROLDE:

Meyering, Jan Roelofs; farmer; age 70; Secessionist; with wife and 1 child; departed 1847.

Roelofs, Cornelus; farmer; age 35; Secessionist; with wife and 2 children; departed 1847.

RUINERWOLD:

Kamer, Jan Roelofs; laborer; age 54; Secessionist; with wife and 2 children; departed 1846.

SLEEN:

Strabbing, Jan; farmer; age 40; Secessionist; with wife and 2 children; departed 1846.

Ensing; maid; age 25; Secessionist; departed 1846.

Uneken (Jantien), widow of R. Rosing; farmer; age 70; Secessionist; with 4 children; departed 1847.

Hunderman, Klaas; farm laborer; age 32; Secessionist; departed 1847.

Stokking, Hindrik; smith; age 38; Reformed; with wife; departed 1847.

Strabbing, Hendrik; farm laborer; age 30; Secessionist; departed 1847.

Strabbing, Mannes; farm laborer; age 27; Secessionist; departed 1847.

Krans, Hindrik; tailor; age 72; Secessionist; with 6 children; departed 1847.

Alting, Jans; farmer; age 30; Secessionist; departed 1847.

Riddering, Jan; farmer; age 59; Secessionist; with wife and 5 children; departed 1847.

Weggemans, Jannes; farmer; age 64; Secessionist; with wife; departed 1847.

Ratering, Teunis; laborer; age 37; Secessionist; with wife and 3 children; departed 1847.

Jalving, Jan; farmer; age 40; Reformed; with wife and 4 children; departed 1847.

Schoemakers, Klaas; farmer; age 32; Secessionist; with wife and 1 child; departed 1847.

Ratering, Gerrit; farmer; age 53; Secessionist; with wife and 6 children; departed 1847.

Lanning, Hendrik; farmer; age 56; Secessionist; with 4 children; departed 1847.

SMILDE:

Nyzing, Jan Willems; farmer; age 36; Secessionist; with wife and 6 children; departed 1847.

Boer, Hendrik Goossens; farmer; age 30; Secessionist; with wife and 4 children; departed 1847.

Stiekel, Hendrik; baker; age 32; Secessionist; departed 1847.

WESTERBORK:

Zwiers, Jan; and his mother; farmer; age 37; Secessionist; with wife and 3 children; departed 1847.

Nyenhuis, Jacob; farmer; age 58; Secessionist; with wife and 3 children; departed 1847.

ZUIDLAREN:

van Rhee, Jan; farmer and carpenter; age 60; Secessionist; with wife, 3 children, and 1 maid; departed 1847.

ZWEELO:

Boes, Jan; farmer and laborer; age 32; Secessionist; with wife; departed 1847.

Euving, Jan; farmer and laborer; age 36; Secessionist; with wife and 3 children; departed 1847.

Kamps, Jan; carpenter; age 26; Secessionist; departed 1847.

Kamps, Fennichje; worker; age 20; Secessionist; departed 1847.

Appendix II[1]

PASSENGER LIST OF THE SOUTHERNER[2]

I, Tully Crosby, do solemnly, sincerely, and truly swear, that the within report and list, subscribed by my name, and now delivered by me to the Collector of the District of New York, contains, to the best of my knowledge and belief, the names, age, sex, and occupation of all the passengers, together with the name of the country to which they severally belong, and that of which they intend to become inhabitants, which were on board the Bark Southerner, whereof I am at present master, at the time of her sailing from the Port of Rotterdam or which have at any time taken on board said vessel. And I do likewise swear, that all matters whatsoever in said Report and List expressed are, to the best of my knowledge and belief, just and true.

Sworn before me this 19th day of November, 1846.

Tully Crosby.

Report and List of Passengers taken on board the Bark Southerner of Boston whereof Tully Crosby is Master, burthen two hundred seventy-six tons and 65/95ths of a ton, bound from the Port of Rotterdam for New York.

NAMES	AGE YEARS	SEX	OCCUPA-TION, TRADE OR PROFESSION	COUNTRY TO WHICH THEY BELONG	COUNTRY THEY INTEND TO BE CITIZENS OF
Jan J. Slotboom	27	male	blacksmith	Netherlands	America
W. P. Slotboom	29	female	none	"	"
Wilhelm B. Slotboom	3½	male	son	"	"
Yohan Slotboom	2	male	son	"	"
S. C. Slotboom	8 mo.	female	daughter	"	"
Frans Smit	44	male	blacksmith	"	"
Gesina Smit	36	female	none	"	"
Geerardus Smit	12	male	son	"	"
Dina Smit	10	female	daughter	"	"
Mina Smit	7	female	daughter	"	"
Jacobus Smit	5	male	son	"	"
Francina Smit	3	female	daughter	"	"
George H. Smit	8 mo.	male	son	"	"
Wouter van den Brink	36	male	carpenter	"	"
Geurtje van der Sande	50	female	none	"	"

81

NAMES	AGE YEARS	SEX	OCCUPA- TION, TRADE OR PROFESSION	COUNTRY TO WHICH THEY BELONG	COUNTRY THEY INTEND TO BE CITIZENS OF
Chrisje van den Brink	18	female	none	"	"
Wouter van der Sande	60	male	farmer	"	"
Leentje Botsen	30	female	none	"	"
Theod Botsen	30	male	farmer	"	"
T. Botsen	1	male	son	"	"
P. A. B. Caspers	30	male	painter	"	"
Rosalie Theresia Briedie	22	female	none	"	"
Henrietta Joseph Caspers	18	female	daughter	"	"
P. C. Olivier	49	male	machinist	"	"
E. G. Olivier	23	male	copperworker	"	"
Amelia Ha. van Supkamp	36	female	none	"	"
W. de Groot	42	male	farmer	"	"
Albert P. Olivier	5	male	son	"	"
Louisa Amelia Olivier	2	female	daughter	"	"
Martend Klaassen	36	male	laborer	"	"
Jan Korten	40	male	laborer	"	"
Geesje Klaassen	45	female	none	"	"
Antonie Korten	10	male	son	"	"
Janna Korten	7	female	daughter	"	"
Gerrit Korten	4	male	son	"	"
Evert Klaassen	33	male	farmer	"	"
Aaltje Jacobs	35	female	none	"	"
Hendrik Jan Klaassen	4	male	son	"	"
Aaltje Klaassen	11 mo.	female	daughter	"	"
Egbert Dunnewind	53	male	farmer	"	"
Tennigse Dunnewind	19	female	none	"	"
Hendrik Dunnewind	13	male	son	"	"
Gerrit Dunnewind	9	male	son	"	"
Evert Dunnewind	8	male	son	"	"
Harm Kok	50	male	farmer	"	"
Janna Dunnewind	47	female	none	"	"
Hermina Kok	20	female	daughter	"	"
Jan Kok	19	male	son	"	"
Hendrik Kok	15	male	son	"	"
Albert Kok	11	male	son	"	"
Martin Kok	9	male	son	"	"
Jan Harm Kok	4	male	son	"	"
H. Jan Kok	1	male	son	"	"
P Bernardus Grotenhuis	32	male	painter	"	"
Janna Hogewind	27	female	none	"	"
Johannes Grotenhuis	5	male	son	"	"
Jacobus Grotenhuis	10 mo.	male	son	"	"
Hendrik Oldemeijer	40	male	farmer	"	"
Dina Schepers	40	female	none	"	"
Jan Oldemeijer	7	male	son	"	"
V Hermannes Lankheet	31	male	miller	"	"
Samuel Korman	26	male	carpenter	"	"
Roelofje Beutem	24	female	none	"	"
Mayelina Korman	7 mo.	female	daughter	"	"

	NAMES	AGE YEARS	SEX	OCCUPATION, TRADE OR PROFESSION	COUNTRY TO WHICH THEY BELONG	COUNTRY THEY INTEND TO BE CITIZENS OF
	Dirk Plasman	48	male	farmer	"	"
	Aaltje Plasman	46	female	none	"	"
	Willem Plasman	18	male	son	"	"
	Fredrik Plasman	11	male	son	"	"
	Jannigje Plasman	8	female	daughter	"	"
	Widow van Zee	63	female	none	"	"
	Mina van Zee	34	female	none	"	"
	Sophia G. van Zee	32	female	none	"	"
	Jan H. Epping van Zee	30	male	blacksmith	"	"
	Johanna van Zee	28	female	none	"	"
	Lubbertus van Zee	26	male	baker	"	"
	Jan Willem van Zee	24	male	baker	"	"
V	Willem Notting	35	male	painter	"	"
V	M. Notting	26	female	none	"	"
	Hendrik Notting	1	male	son	"	"
	Widow Laarman	60	female	none	"	"
V	Jan Laarman	30	male	son farmer	"	"
	Geesje Laarman	25	female	none	"	"
	Jan Hendrik Laarman	1½	male	son	"	"
	Albert Notting	11	male	son	"	"
V	Evert Zagers	32	male	weaver	"	"
	Roelofje Vrielink (Died Oct. 16 — inflammation of bowels)	40	female	none	"	"
	Hendrik Zagers	5	male	son	"	"
V	Egbert Fredriks	31	male	laborer	"	"
	Anna Harms	27	female	none	"	"
	Roelofje Fredriks (Died Nov. 1 — dropsy, sick)	2	female	daughter	"	"
	Geesje Fredriks	12 mo. 9 weeks	female	daughter	"	"
	T. van den Boogaard	28	female	tailor	"	"
	Maria van den Boogaard	30	female	none	"	"
	Lena van den Boogaard	3	female	daughter	"	"
	Elisabeth van den Boogaard (Died Oct. 13 — sick when left port)	11 mo.	female	daughter	"	"
	Casper Schneider	25	male	workman	"	"
	T. van Estorick	39	male	painter	"	"
	G. Blom	39	male	tailor	"	"
	H. de Kruyf	29	male	farmer	"	"
	Bernard Ebbeling	22	male	wooden shoes	"	"
	G. F. Westerhout (Left at Rotterdam on eve of sailing)	33	male	merchant	"	"
	Aartje Karsman	21	female	servant	"	"

NAMES	AGE YEARS	SEX	OCCUPA-TION, TRADE OR PROFESSION	COUNTRY TO WHICH THEY BELONG	COUNTRY THEY INTEND TO BE CITIZENS OF
		CABIN PASSENGERS			
V A. C. Van Raalte	35	male	clergyman	"	"
Johanna Christina Van Raalte	32	female	none	"	"
Albertus Van Raalte	9	male	son	"	"
Johanna Maria Van Raalte	7	female	daughter	"	"
Benjamin Van Raalte	5	male	son	"	"
Dirk Van Raalte	2	male	son	"	"
Christina Catharine Van Raalte	5 mo.	female	daughter	"	"
Tennigje Lasker	40	female	servant	"	"

NOTES

1. Supplied by Mr. Willard Wichers of the Netherlands Information Bureau in Holland, Michigan, through the courtesy of Prof. Dr. Albert Hyma (University of Michigan).

2. I have italicized the names of the people who came from the province of Drenthe. It is noteworthy that they are listed together; they apparently formed a separate group when the list was drawn up. Of the 109 people who sailed, 22 were from Drenthe, that is, twenty percent. The pioneers of the famous Vanguard to Holland, Michigan, are marked with a V; that is, the Reverend van Raalte and 6 of his followers. Of these 7 ("the small band of heroes," according to van Hinte), 6 were from Drenthe—that is, eighty-three percent! Besides the Vanguard, B. Grootenhuis (P) deserves special mention. Counting him, the people from Drenthe form seventy-one percent. (The number of children of Widow van Zee and Widow Laarman does not correspond to the count in *Appendix* I; did some die even before they sailed?)